Daily

Guide to BUYING *and* SELLING Your HOME

Daily Mail Guide to Buying and Selling Your Home

Edited by Margaret Stone

The Daily Mail's award winning team of 'Money Mail' personal finance writers, Wendy Elkington, Wayne Asher, Rosanna Spero and James Hopegood, have pooled their specialist knowledge here to provide the essential guide to house-buying.

Starting with the basic question Why buy?, this accessible guide is packed with down-to-earth advice and useful tips on:

- choosing a property
- negotiating a price
- making the offer
- exchanging contracts
- preparing for the move
- how your mortgage works
- insurance and paying the bills
- making alteratiuons and improvements.

There are also chapters devoted to selling your home, buying in Scotland and building your home.

If you are buying for the first time or looking to move another rung up the housing ladder, this practical guide will help you enter the house-buying maze with confidence.

Daily Mail Guide to BUYING *and* SELLING Your HOME

Edited by
Margaret Stone

Contributors: Wendy Elkington, Rosanna Spero,
Wayne Asher and James Hopegood

KOGAN
PAGE

First published in 1997

Kogan Page Limited
120 Pentonville Road
London N1 9JN

British Library Cataloguing in Publication Data

A CIP record for this book is available from the British Library.

ISBN 0 7494 2378 1

Typeset by Saxon Graphics Ltd, Derby
Printed and bound in Great Britain by Thanet Press Ltd
Illustrations by John Plumb

CONTENTS

FOREWORD

OWNING your own home is a particularly British preoccupation. We have one of the highest levels of owner-occupation in the world, and our appetite for home ownership has hardly been diminished by the well-publicised problems that house-buyers faced at the height of the recession in the early 1990s.

Most young people today know couples, families and single men and women who got their fingers badly burned when the housing market collapsed at this time. But, survey after survey shows that their personal long-term ambition is to own their own property.

There are significant advantages to owning your own home. You can be flexible in your choice of property – a semi, flat, bungalow or thatched cottage – and just as flexible in location. You can live in the country, in the heart of the city, or close to the school you want your children to attend. You can even build your own home.

Of course, today's house-buyers will be wiser than the generation which rushed recklessly into house purchase in the late 1980s. Excessive borrowing coupled with crazy house prices have left an unhappy legacy of negative equity for, at its peak, over 2 million house-holders, and repossessions were the worst the lending industry had ever experienced.

But I believe that the lessons have been learned. No borrowers, whether first-time buyers or families moving to their next house, should borrow more they can comfortably afford – ideally with a little to spare. A sudden rise in mortgage interest rates can completely upset the calculations of house-buyers who have borrowed up to the hilt.

But with the economy on the upturn and confidence returning, the upswing in the housing market is becoming more solidly based. Families are looking forward to trading up into a bigger property and those who are renting are gearing themselves up to become first-time buyers. For many of them it will be a cheaper option – and they will have something to show for it at the end.

Homes are for living in. This is the principal reason for buying your own dream house, flat or bungalow. In the past, house-buyers have made a substantial profit out of their bricks and mortar. Sadly, a later generation have lost out as their homes have dropped in value. There is nothing wrong if your house turns out to be a good investment and you make some money out of it. But remember, first and foremost, it is your home.

'Money Mail', the weekly personal finance section of the *Daily Mail*, was the first of its kind in the national press and remains a leader. It has always provided readers with guidance and insight into the housing market. Articles on borrowing, the most suitable types of mortgage for different categories of home-buyers, house insurance and dealing with the legal and tax implications of home ownership are very popular.

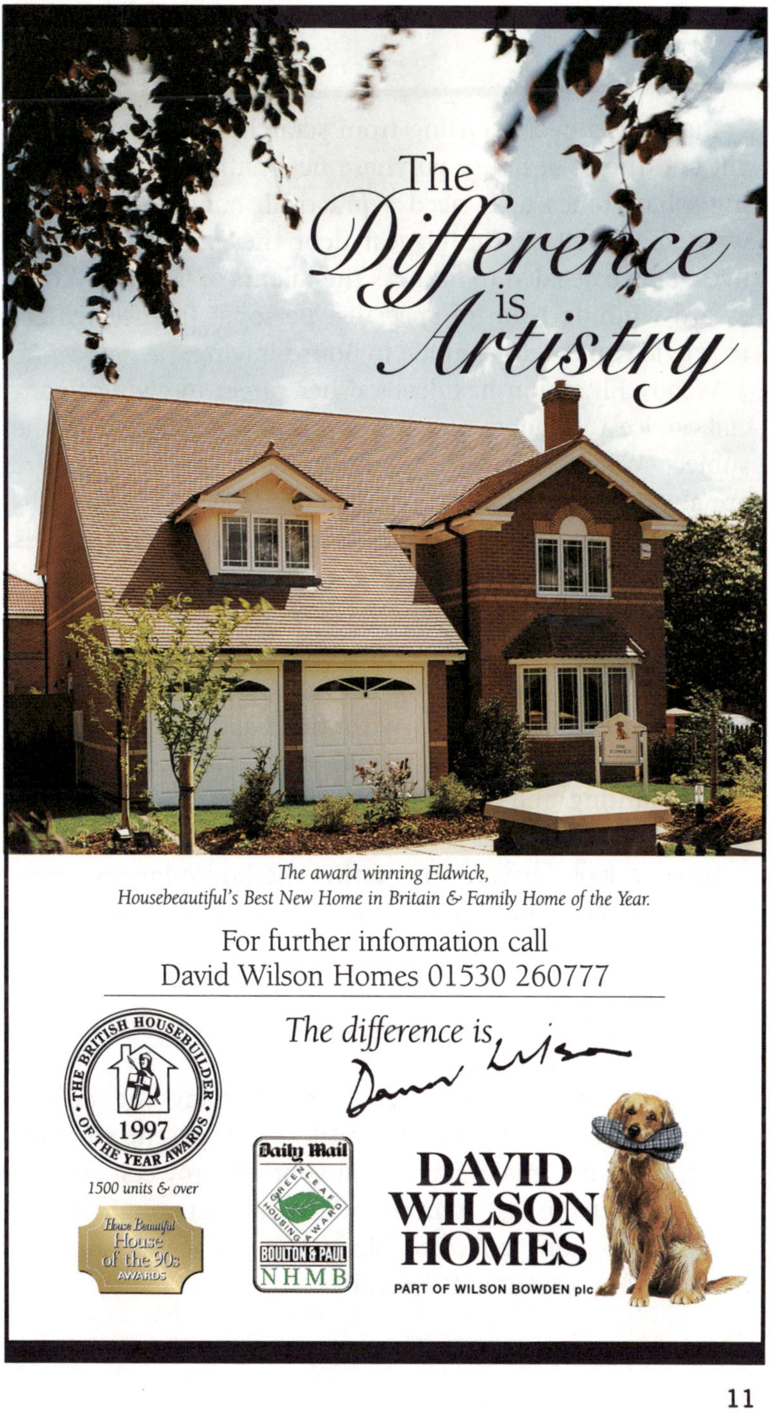
The Difference is Artistry
The award winning Eldwick,
Housebeautiful's Best New Home in Britain & Family Home of the Year.
For further information call
David Wilson Homes 01530 260777
The difference is
THE BRITISH HOUSEBUILDER OF THE YEAR AWARDS
1997
1500 units & over
House Beautiful
House of the 90s
AWARDS
Daily Mail
GREENLEAF HOUSING AWARD
BOULTON & PAUL
NHMB
DAVID WILSON HOMES
PART OF WILSON BOWDEN plc

But housebuyers starting from scratch or engaged in the cut and thrust of house purchase negotiations and wondering what comes next need a practical, hands on guide to what may well be the biggest debt they take on in their lives. So we decided to harness the talents of 'Money Mail's' award-winning team of specialist personal finance writers to provide an essential guide to house-buying.

Wendy Elkington has devoted her career to giving financial advice to readers and has written many books on the subject. Wayne Asher is on hand to make sure that readers are always given a fair deal and James Hopegood's speciality is mortgage finance, while Rosanna Spero concentrates on insurance matters.

This book is for those who have made up their minds to buy, or are looking to move another rung up the housing ladder. In easily accessible form, it gives a complete guide to home ownership, starting with the basic question: why buy? It is packed with tips to take with you when you start house-hunting and start to narrow down the choice to a selected few properties.

You can look forward to entering the house-buying maze with confidence and there are special sections to help buyers who are brave enough to buy at auction – there's no pulling back! – or who are buying in Scotland where different rules apply, which, among other things, safeguard the house-buyer from gazumping.

There is a strong argument for reforming the house-buying process in England and Wales. The present arrangement does not really favour anyone. Borrowers can be gazumped at the last minute; sellers can get caught in an impossible chain; unacceptable delays are commonplace; and heartbreak is often the result.

From time to time, a head of steam builds up and attempts are made to sort out the unsatisfactory way in which we are forced to buy our homes. Sadly, it usually runs out. In the meantime, housebuyers will have to put up with the current system. This book is designed to give you the upper hand at every stage in your quest to own that house of your dreams.

Margaret Stone, Editor, 'Money Mail'

1

WHY BUY?

THERE comes a point in most people's lives when, fed up with paying someone else's mortgage, they decide to put down roots and buy their own home.

The UK is unusual in Europe in that over two-thirds of the population own their own home, compared with just over a third in Germany and just over half in France. The number of owner-occupiers has grown steadily since the Second World War, when less than one in three people owned the homes they lived in. Now only 7 per cent of people rent from a private landlord, with local councils and housing associations making up the remaining 25 per cent.

There are many advantages in owning your own home:

- **You have greater choice of property and location**

  You can choose any architectural style – a newly-built home, a Victorian conversion or a terraced house, for example. And you can choose the exact location you want to live in rather than be dictated to by where rental property is available and affordable.

- **More choice of public and private facilities such as schools, shops and public transport**

  Depending on your age, different facilities take priority. For example, a family with young children may choose where they live for the local schools or access to parks and leisure centres. For older people, peace and quiet may become a priority or, for those without a car, good public transport.

- **Security of tenure**

  The great thing about owning your own home is that you cannot be moved out at the whim of a landlord. The only way that you can be forced to move once you own a property is if you fall behind with mortgage payments and your home is repossessed by the building society.

- **A hedge against inflation**

  One of the main reasons why people buy property is that they hope the value of their home will rise at least in line with the cost of living – inflation. So, when they want to sell, the price they get is the same in real terms, after inflation has been taken into account, as the one they paid for it – if not higher. Before the collapse of the housing market in the late 1980s – early 1990s, most people expected the value of their house to far outstrip what they paid for it. After several years of negative equity – when the value of the house fell below the level of the mortgage loan – people have scaled down their expectations.

- **Mortgage tax relief – MIRAS**

  Home ownership has been encouraged by giving

borrowers tax relief on the interest they pay on their home loans. Originally borrowers obtained tax relief at their top rate of tax on the interest on the entire loan. But this attraction has been steadily whittled away. Mortgage interest relief is now given at one level – 15 per cent – and only on the first £30,000 of the loan. The relief is usually built into the mortgage payments – hence the acronym MIRAS, which stands for mortgage interest relief at source. Although greatly reduced, the tax relief is still worth having as it does reduce monthly payments by about £27.17 a month when interest rates are at 7.25 per cent.

- **Freedom to modify and decorate your home to your own personal tastes**

  Once you own a property you can redecorate exactly as you wish – if pink walls and purple carpet is your idea of heaven, there is no landlord to impose restrictions on you. Outside, things can get a bit more complicated. Any extensions or major changes will probably require planning permission and, depending on where you live, there may be some rules governing the colour of the exterior of the house.

- **Often a cheaper monthly outlay than in equivalent rented accommodation**

  This has only become true in the past few years. For much of the 1980s, the opposite was true. But while interest rates are low, and the stock of good quality rented accommodation is limited, home owners will continue to find that it is cheaper to buy than rent.

There are, of course, down sides to owning your own home:

- **You are responsible for all the bills**

  In most rented accommodation the landlord will pay the water bill and sometimes the service charge if the flat is part of a block. The landlord is also responsible for any maintenance costs, the buildings insurance and a portion of the home contents insurance (covering any furniture already in the flat when you moved in). When you own your own home you must pay for all repairs, insurance and bills.

- **You are responsible for meeting the mortgage costs**

  The vast majority of mortgages must be paid monthly and it is the responsibility of the home owner to make sure that this happens. If it does not, the lender is allowed to repossess the home and can usually chase you for the money. If you fall behind on rent you can also be booted out and chased for the money, but you will lose any money you have invested in the home, if you have done so.

- **The prospect that mortgage costs might rise**

  Once you own your own home, you are committed to paying off the mortgage regardless of whether interest rates rise. This caused enormous problems in the 1980s, when people mortgaged themselves up to the hilt and then could not afford the repayments when interest rates began to rise. If you are buying, make sure you can afford any rise in interest rates. Despite the recent recession, house prices have grown by 1.7 per cent each year in real terms since 1950 and in 1996 alone they grew by around 7 per cent according to the Halifax, the country's largest mortgage lender. The average house price recorded in December 1996 was £66,831. But this figure can be broken down further: first-time buyers paid an average price of £48,167, while the figure for other borrowers moving into their next property was £76,755. The average price of a new house was £69,212.

For home-buyers, the cost of housing has traditionally been their biggest monthly outlay. At the end of 1996, £25.60 of every £100 earned went goes on housing, says the TSB banking group. This figure is set to rise over the next year and the TSB predicts that by the end of 1997 the cost per £100 will rise to £30.70.

The benefits of owning your own property often require a long-term view, as they may take time to become apparent:

- **It allows you to build up equity**

  Despite the setback in the housing market in recent years, the majority of home owners expect that the value of their home will increase and provide 'profit' over the purchase price. This free share in your home is a valuable asset, usually referred to as the 'equity' in your house. Its value is real – for example, if you want to borrow money to help start a business, banks are usually willing to lend you money against the equity in your home.

- **You can use the enhanced value of your property**

  You can trade up and move into a larger home; or you could move into a more expensive neighbourhood.

- **You can trade down to a smaller house**

  This releases some of the capital tied up in your house to use as you wish, particularly as you get older – perhaps for a retirement trip around the world or investing for extra income to improve your pension.

- **Home income plans**

  These enable the elderly to unlock the capital in their home without them having to move out.

- **For the elderly, a home can be used to help meet the needs of long term care**

  The government is considering special schemes which will enable older people to borrow against part of the value of their house to help meet nursing home or care fees.

- **Benefiting the next generation**

  Many people are pleased that the rising value of their home gives them a valuable asset to leave to their children.

- **Community involvement**

  Owning your own home gives you a stake in society and the wellbeing of your community that might otherwise be absent.

RENTING VERSUS BUYING

One of the biggest factors in deciding whether to buy or rent is the cost. During the 1980s, the cost of renting was lower than the cost of buying, and tenants had the freedom to move areas and homes cheaply and easily, while home owners had to go through the lengthy buying and selling process before they could follow suit.

But the relative costs have changed in the last few years and since the early 1990s it has been cheaper to own your own home than to rent. According to figures from stockbroker and research house UBS the crossover came in late 1992 and will only be reversed when mortgage rates and house prices rise. Add to this the fact that the availability of good rented accommodation, especially in the major cities, is low and the case for becoming an owner-occupier becomes stronger.

Few would dispute that now (1997) is, from the economic point of view, the perfect time to buy:

- Mortgage rates are still relatively low and the cost of housing is rising steadily rather than spiralling out of control

- Buying and owning a property is also ideally suited to the current low inflation environment

It means that as the cost of borrowing is low potential house-buyers are able to afford larger mortgages than they could if interest rates were high.

When the rate of inflation is high, property prices might rise quickly, but so too could interest rates – thus increasing the cost of a mortgage.

- There are more different types of mortgages available than ever before. For example, if you are intending to take out a large mortgage it might be worth looking at some of the fixed rate mortgages

But owning your own property is not always easy. In the second half of 1993 alone, some 193,660 home owners were three to six months in arrears on their mortgage and 151,810 were more than six months behind. In the first half of 1996, some 24,100 of the 10.591 million home owners in the UK had their houses repossessed. The figures have fallen as house prices have risen, but in the same period of 1996 there were still 348,580 home owners more than three months behind with their mortgages.

The main reason for the high level of arrears was the frenzy of borrowing in the 1980s when people were able, and encouraged, to mortgage themselves to the hilt. When interest rates rose – peaking at 15.4 per cent in 1990 – many people could not afford the monthly repayments and so had to sell their homes. If there was a shortfall between the selling price and the amount of the loan, ex-home owners were also forced to find the money to make up the shortfall.

Fuelled by the easy availability of credit, house prices reached dizzy levels and people were often paying well above the realistic value of the property. It can only be hoped that in the current house price boom, home owners will have learnt their lesson and will not overextend themselves with mortgages they cannot afford if interest rates rise.

HOME OWNERSHIP TRENDS

The main reasons for the changing patterns of home ownership have been increasing affluence and tax incentives. The Housing Acts of 1980 and 1984 allowed local authorities to sell their housing stock to tenants for heavily discounted prices and sales of these homes rose from 92,000 in 1980 to a peak of 228,000 in 1982.

Unfortunately, many of the people who bought under these 'right to buy' schemes are now experiencing problems. Many properties have become virtually unsaleable. In some cases, they are one of only a few properties actually owner-occupied on a council estate. In others, mortgage lenders now say that they are unhappy with some of the construction methods used and are refusing to lend to potential buyers.

Many of the major lenders are now refusing to lend to potential home owners wanting to buy in high rise blocks – and in some cases this is classified as ones with more than four storeys. Problems are also being experienced by people wanting to buy flats above shops, and even studio or one-bedroom flats within a house.

HOUSE PRICES

The price of homes is influenced by two simple factors – supply and demand. But within this it gets more complex.

There is still a shortage of suitable housing in many areas of Britain including London, the South East and East Anglia, while some northern towns have a surplus – especially where the area has suffered industrial decline – and home owners are finding it difficult to sell at any price.

According to the Halifax Building Society, house prices in Northern Ireland grew by 13.9 per cent in 1996 against 5.6 per cent in the North West, 5 per cent in Yorkshire and Humberside and 6.2 per cent in the West Midlands. The highest house price inflation in 1996, however, was experienced in Greater London where prices rose by 14.9 per cent.

These regional variations can be seen in the cost of an average semi-detached home in the last quarter of 1996. A house-buyer in Barnsley, South Yorkshire, paid just £43,200, while in Harrogate, North Yorkshire, an equivalent property cost £65,450. Someone buying in Basingstoke, Hampshire, paid £80,700, while Ipswich house-buyers paid £54,100. The two most expensive areas were London at £167,350 and St Albans at £115,350, while Doncaster, South Yorkshire, was the cheapest at £38,200.

INFLUENCES ON HOUSE PRICES

Location is not the only factor influencing house prices. It also comes down to the individual properties. Issues such as the size of the property, the type – flat, house, terraced, semi-detached or detached – as well as the general repair and standard of decor will also play a big part.

There are also several major interest groups which will influence the cost of a home. These are central government, local government and the property profession, including architects, chartered surveyors, estate agents and house builders.

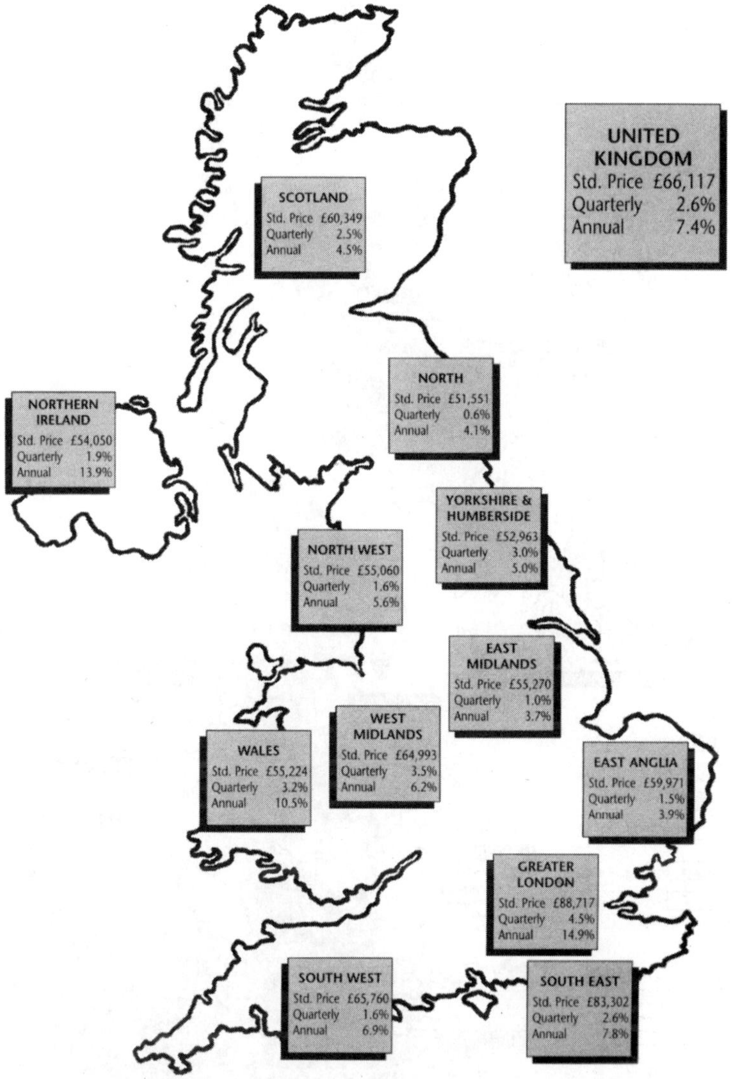

Percentage changes are based on Regional Standardised Indices of House Prices (All Houses, All Buyers, Seasonally Adjusted) and relate to the change over the last quarter (Quarterly) and the same quarter a year ago (Annual).

Source: *Halifax*

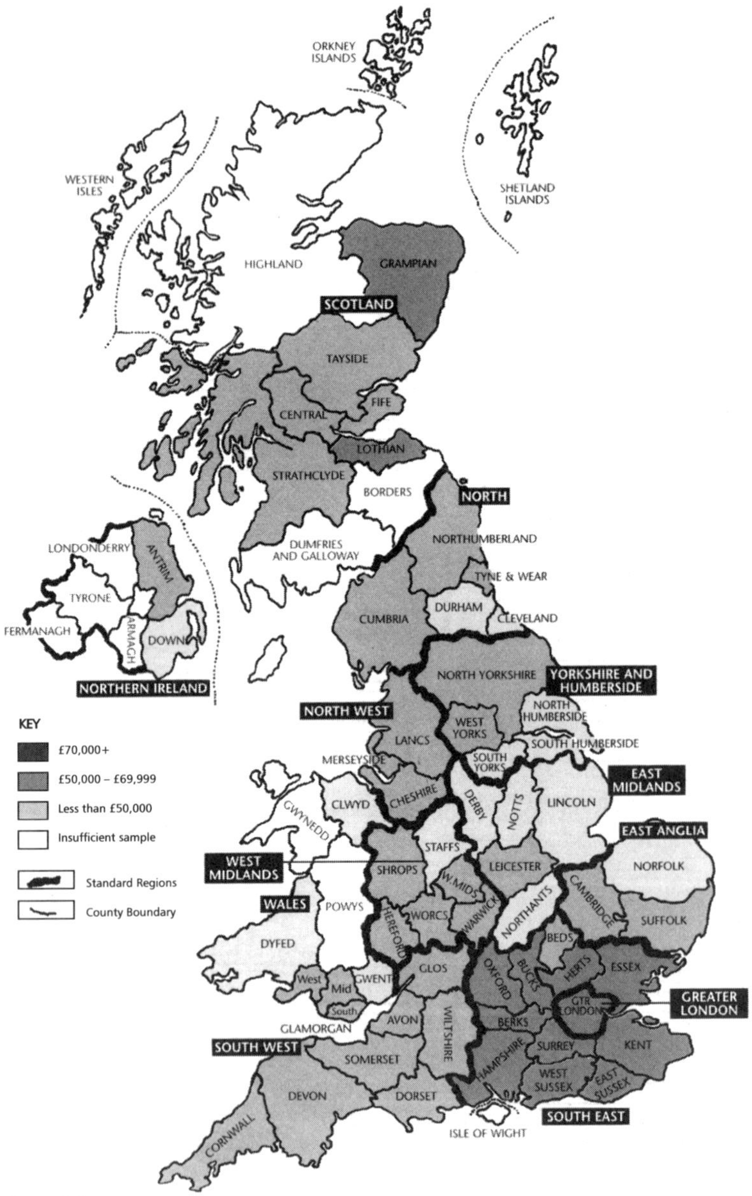

Source: *Halifax*

Central government and local government

Major and minor legislation can have a severe effect on property values. It is usually the local authority which is charged with implementing the law.

- Major housing policy – such as permitting council tenants to buy their homes under the 'right to buy' provisions and alterations to leasehold law, which are enabling more people to buy the freeholds of their homes
- Housing finance and improvement policy – such as the reduction in mortgage interest tax relief and limiting its application to fewer borrowers
- Housing land policy and major planning issues – such as the restrictions on planning development in green belt areas or the devastating effect of a motorway or proposed new rail line on a village

The property profession

The property roll call includes many professions and industries whose members can have an impact on individual properties and areas, and to some extent influence house prices. It is worth being aware of the role each of these groups plays as it is often in their interest to talk up the housing market, and their statements on the subject are likely to have an effect on property prices.

- Chartered surveyors – carry out the valuation of properties, property management, structural surveys and oversee new developments. Their valuation of a property can knock thousands of pounds off the selling price of a property

- Estate agents – carry out the valuation of property, negotiation, selling of property, housing finance and complete relocation packages. An unofficial aspect of their job is to demonstrate confidence in the housing market and talk up the value of individual properties

- Architects – design and layout of new homes and improvements and extensions to existing ones

- House builders – the amount and price of new properties being built will demonstrate confidence in the area, and new house prices help set the price of older, established homes

- Banks, building societies and other lenders – can have a major influence on the housing market by providing finance for both individuals and developers

- Insurance companies – are involved in the financing and development of housing, but their impact is usually too remote to have much effect on house prices

REMEMBER ...

- Buying your own home gives you complete freedom to choose the property and location which are perfect for you
- You can choose to live close to the local amenities which suit your lifestyle
- Buying can often be cheaper than renting, especially with the current scarcity of rented accommodation
- You will enjoy greater security and there can be financial advantages – your home can be an investment

BUT

- You will have sole responsibility for the mortgage and all the bills – make sure your budget can stand it
- Interest rates can rise as well as fall and you will need to allow yourself a little financial leeway
- Economically, now is the perfect time to buy – but to be sure of gaining financially from your home, you must be prepared for a long-term commitment

2

HOUSE-HUNTING

BUYING a house is probably the biggest purchase anyone makes in their lifetime, so it makes sense to do some serious forward planning before you start.

The first thing to decide is exactly where you want to live. Visit the area and walk or drive round it looking at the different character of each street and assessing the amenities around it. Talk to people who live locally to get a feel for the place. It may be worth drawing an outline on a map indicating the street or group of streets you would like to live in.

Find out about council tax charges if you are looking at properties in two different, but adjacent, local authorities. There could be a substantial variation which might influence your choice of area.

It is also worth writing a checklist of the amenities and issues that are important to you:

- Set the maximum amount you can afford to pay and don't be tempted to go above it. Remember that mortgage interest rates fluctuate, so work out if you could still afford the monthly payments if rates rose by 5 per cent, for example. Go and see a lender to get a loan agreed in principle. Chapters 7 and 8 deal with mortgages in detail

- Are you looking to buy a flat, maisonette or house? This may seem obvious, but think about the increased bills moving from a flat to a house: can you afford them? Do you have enough furniture? Or, if moving from a house to a flat, what will you do with the extra furniture that you no longer have room for?
- If you want a house, do you want a terraced, semi-detached or detached one? Also are you looking for an old or a newly built property?
- If you have or are planning to have children, what are the nurseries and schools like in the area? How easy are they to get to?

- Do you want a garden, or would a nearby park be adequate?
- Is public transport important? If yes, how close do you want buses, tubes or trains to be?
- Do you want a garage, or are you happy with street parking?

Once you have decided where you want to live, all you have to do is find your dream property. House-hunting is a time-consuming and frustrating process. Unless you are remarkably lucky, you will have to forgo many weekends and some evenings in your quest for your new home. Give yourself as much of a head start as possible by making use of all the services and agencies available to you.

ESTATE AGENTS

A list of all the local firms can be found in Yellow Pages or the local Thomson directory. Although most agents sell a wide range of properties, they do try to establish themselves in their own market niche. Some will specialise in first-time buyer properties whilst others will deal in more expensive properties. Visit their offices and register with the ones who are able to offer your type of home.

In addition to acting as negotiator between buyer and seller, most are keen to offer mortgage finance and even life insurance to both parties. The agent will be very keen to know if you are involved in a chain or are a cash buyer. Try to establish a relationship. This is very important in a tight market, as if the agent knows you are really serious, you may get first chance to see a property which has just come on the market. If you have access to a fax, arrange for the details to be sent to you immediately they are available.

HOUSE-HUNTING FROM A DISTANCE

If you are moving to a completely new area, work commitments may make house-hunting difficult. Many agents do belong to large networks and their local office may be able to supply you with helpful introductions. The National Association of Estate Agents operates a Homelink service which is likely to have contacts with other Homelink members in the area to which you are moving.

A good agent should be able to save you a lot of unnecessary footwork and wasted journeys by eliminating unsuitable properties. But it is definitely worth spending a few days in your new area to get a feel for the area and the local colour.

- Free property newspapers: these are published in many areas and distributed free by local agents and shops
- Newspaper adverts: many people object to paying estate agents' fees and advertise their property privately in the local press. It can be worthwhile placing an order with a newsagent to make sure you get your copy on time. There are also specialist magazines such as *Daltons Weekly* and *Exchange and Mart*
- Relocation agencies: although most agencies tend to specialise in relocation for company employees, many firms will now work on behalf of individuals who do not have the time to devote to house-hunting. Many agencies are members of the Association of Relocation Agents

- Repossessions: you can obtain lists from estate agents and auctions of such properties and they are often advertised in the local press.
- Your own advertisement: use the 'wanted' column in the property section of the local newspaper. Make sure you paint the full picture so that you get suitable replies
- Get on your bike: Arm yourself with a local street map and hunt out the estate agents' boards which indicate that a property is for sale

WHAT DO YOU WANT IN A HOUSE?

Buying a property is generally a compromise. You have to be extremely fortunate to find everything you want but it is worthwhile making a checklist of those features which are important to you. Here are some important guidelines:

- Size – is it big enough – or even small enough? Look to the future – are there enough bedrooms if you are planning a family? Will you have relations coming to stay regularly – perhaps you may have to look after an elderly relative? Do you want to let out a room to help pay the mortgage? Do you need an extra room for office space?
- Rooms – are they the right size? Do you need extra space for kids to play or do their homework? High Victorian ceilings look impressive but are costly to heat. Is there enough space for entertaining? Do you need a second or en-suite bathroom to avoid the early

morning queue and is there a separate lavatory? Are the rooms suitable for your furniture?

- Kitchen – very often the focal point of the house. Is it the right size and does the layout suit you? Will you have to modernise it? Are there enough power points and will your own equipment fit in? Is there a separate utility room?
- Entrance – is it grand enough for you? Which way does the door face and is there a protective porch? Can you get your furniture through the entrance and up the stairs?
- Garage – will your car fit and is access easy? Is there space for other family cars? If there is no garage, how about off-street parking? Is parking easy in the street?
- Garden – which way does it face and how much sun does it get? Is it big enough for the kids to play in – and are there any danger points such as a pond or tall trees? Do you really need a large garden with all the work it entails?
- Heating – does it have central heating and, if so, what type – gas is generally considered cheaper than electric? How old is the boiler and are the radiators old-fashioned? Open fires look romantic, but they can be difficult to keep clean. There may be clean air regulations in force in urban areas
- General – does the house feel damp? A survey will show if there are any problems. Are there any shared facilities such as party walls? Do the windows let in lots of light? Remember that an empty house without

curtains can sometimes appear brighter than a room which is fully furnished

These are just a few of the more important angles which you should consider. As your search continues, other pieces will fall into place in the house-hunting jigsaw. One good tip is to always carry a notepad, pen and tape measure so that you can keep a record of your ideas and questions.

NEW OR OLD?

We have a very mature housing stock in this country and buyers have an enormous choice, ranging from a small terraced cottage, or a substantial semi-detached, up to a country mansion. But new houses are being added to this stock all the time and there can be many advantages in buying a recently-built house.

The advantages of buying a new house are:

- There are schemes available which protect the buyer against structural defects. The most popular is run by the National House Building Council (NHBC), which has a 10-year Buildmark warranty. During the first two years of a property's existence, any defects have to be put right by the builder at no cost to the buyer. For the next eight years, an insurance policy covers major damage caused by structural defects
- Materials will generally be of a higher standard. Insulation is normally better and future maintenance costs should be negligible. Kitchens and electrical

fitments will be modern and double glazing may be fitted as standard

- If you buy the house before it is completed, you will be able to choose many of the fixtures and fittings to co-ordinate with your own design. For example, you may be able to influence the kitchen layout as well as the colour of the bathroom
- You will not have to cope with the lapses of taste of the previous owners who will have installed their own ideas and colour schemes
- Maintenance costs can be lower than on an older house, where insulation and heating bills could also be a lot higher
- You will not be involved in any chain on the purchase side. Some builders offer to buy your existing property to boost sales
- It is normally easier to get a mortgage on a new house. Some builders have special arrangements with building societies and sometimes 100 per cent loans are available
- There may be incentives to buy, such as a price reduction if contracts are exchanged within a certain period
- If you are finding it difficult to sell your present home, some builders will buy it from you to enable you to buy one of their new homes. The price (reached after consultation with several estate agents) may not be quite as high as you might have hoped, but you will not be stuck in a home you no longer want

The drawbacks of moving into a new home:

- New houses can be lacking in character, may not be built in an established area and many modern housing estates have a degree of 'sameness'
- It may cost more to finish off than you think. For example, you may have to buy extras such as light fittings, curtains and rails and cupboards as well as landscaping the garden
- There are bound to be running-in problems – known as snagging in the trade – which the builder will have to put right
- Rooms and gardens tend to be smaller than in older properties, as space is generally at a premium
- The price of a new house tends to be higher than for a similar older property and it may take a while before you get your money back
- You may have to pay for the property in stage payments while it is being built and still repay the mortgage on your present house
- The house may not be finished on time, which could lead to difficulties and extra costs on the sale of your existing property
- There is less room to bargain on prices than with an older property
- There is less opportunity to make a profit on renovation

HOME OWNERSHIP

Property can be bought either on a freehold or a leasehold basis. Freehold gives you absolute ownership of the property

and the land on which it stands and is the most usual form of 'tenure'. But many residential properties which go on sale are still leasehold.

It means that ultimately the property will return to the person or company which granted the lease. In practical terms this can still give a great deal of security as most long leases are for 99 years and can be as long as 999 years. However, as the unexpired period of the lease reduces, the value of the property may also diminish.

Leaseholds generally apply to flats, whether purpose-built or house conversions. The details of the lease will include service agreements, annual charges and any restrictions placed on the use of the property – called restrictive covenants. In addition, leaseholders pay an annual ground rent to the landlord.

There has been a variety of legislation over the last 30 years to protect leaseholders and give them more security, including the right to extend their lease, or even buy the freehold. This has culminated in the 1993 Leasehold Reform, Housing and Urban Development Act which gives three important rights to leaseholders:

- Collective enfranchisement – this simply means that, subject to certain qualifying conditions, flat owners can appoint a representative to buy the freehold on behalf of the tenants
- Lease renewal – flat owners can now renew their leases for a further 90 years, once they have been living in the flat for two years
- Management audit – owners may appoint a surveyor to make sure the block is being managed properly

One of the limiting factors on new-style freehold flats is that there may be problems in raising a mortgage. As yet, many lenders have not worked out a system which takes into account the possibility that there may be different types of ownership within the block. For example, some owners may have bought their freehold, whilst others are content to remain with the original lease.

The Leasehold Enfranchisement Advisory Service (LEAS) (0171 493 3116) can give advice on leasehold problems.

OTHER TYPES OF OWNERSHIP

- Local authority: tenants of council property who have lived there for three years or more have the right to buy at a substantial discount
- Housing association: enables purchasers to buy a share in a house. For example, if their finances do not allow outright purchase, they are able to buy an initial share of, perhaps, one quarter. The rest is then rented and, as finances improve, it is possible to increase the share to the full 100 per cent. The Housing Corporation can provide full details. See Chapter 7 on shared ownership
- Mobile homes: although cheaper to buy, there are hidden costs. Normally, there are expensive ground rents to pay and a fixed percentage is often deducted by the owner of the land whenever a mobile home is sold

REMEMBER ...

- Get to know the area – look around, read the local papers, speak to local people
- This 'grass roots' approach could help you find a house, too – don't forget, there are other resources besides your estate agent
- Check the level of council tax in the area
- Write yourself a list of important considerations: your price limit (allowing for interest rate fluctuations); the kind of property you're looking for; whether you need to be near a school or any other amenities; whether you want a garden or a garage
- Do you want to buy a new or an old property?
- Do you want to buy freehold or leasehold? From a private seller, a local authority or a housing association?
- Don't sacrifice any vital requirements, but be willing to compromise when necessary

3

VIEWING PROPERTIES

ACTUALLY viewing the properties is one of the hardest parts of the buying process and it is advisable to see only one or two at any one time, otherwise you are likely to get confused and muddle one up with another.

The first time you go and see a property, don't try and take in all the smallest details; they can be assessed on a return visit. It is also worth viewing a property with a friend or spouse, both because they may be able to point out features or defects that you have missed and also for your own personal security.

If you are visiting a property on your own, make sure you tell someone where you are going and at what time, so they can raise the alarm if you are not back within a reasonable time.

Wander round the property, preferably alone – although an estate agent or owner may insist on coming with you – and get a feel for the place. Is the place light and airy? Remember, an empty property will look lighter than it will actually be once it has curtains, carpets and furniture in it. Do you like the size and layout of the rooms and do you get a good feel for the place?

Once you have visited a few properties, you will begin to get a feel for what you like and dislike and will be able to narrow your list down to the ones you want to return to. Do not be sidetracked by the price or the sales pitch of the estate agent – it is ultimately you who has to live in the house so it has to be right for you and not just a bargain.

When you view a property for the first time it is worth taking a notebook with you to jot down impressions, room sizes and particular likes and dislikes so you can compare it against others that you visit. Don't let the decor put you off: that can easily be remedied with a coat of paint. Use your imagination to see what the rooms would look like with your colour scheme and furniture.

If you decide you like a property and want to revisit it, then it is worth doing some more serious homework before you go. Sit down and write out a detailed checklist to tick off as you view each room. Remember that the outside is as important as the interior.

It is important to visit the house you are interested in at different times of day. Visiting it between five and seven in the evening will give a good indication of traffic levels and noise, while earlier in the afternoon will allow you to see how much light the house gets – or discover how noisy children at the local school can be.

OUTSIDE

This is a checklist covering the external features of the house. These tend to get neglected – which is a mistake.

- The situation and location of the property – is it on a main road, near a busy junction where cars are con-

Talk to us first

Photograph shows one of Persimmon Homes' South East developments.

Whether a first time buyer or looking for your fifth home, our professional sales advisers make moving a pleasure - we have a wide range of homes across the South East and would be delighted to welcome you. If you are interested in any area not listed in the South East, please telephone our regional office on 01932-350555 as we are continually opening new developments.

WOKING
'Acorn Vale'
2,3 & 4 bedroom homes
£81,500-£195,000
Tel 01483 489966

'Oakwood Copse'
2 bedroom apartments from
£68,950
Tel 01483 474635

CHISWICK
'Corney Reach'
3 & 4 bedroom town houses
£249,950-£419,950
Tel 0181 742 7477
2 bedroom apartments coming soon

SOUTHWATER
'Ghyll Meadows'
2,3 & 4 bedroom homes
£71,950-£148,000
Tel 01403 732966

NORTHUMBERLAND HEATH
'Northumberland Park'
3 & 4 bedroom homes from
£86,500
1 bedroom apartments from
£45,950
Tel 01322 342857

EPSOM
'Abelea Green'
3 & 4 bedroom detached homes from
£156,500
5 bedroom homes coming soon

BURGESS HILL
'The Oaks'
3 & 4 bedroom homes
£98,000-£146,000
Tel 01444 257218

HORSHAM
'Tanbridge Park'
4 bedroom homes from
£158,000
2 bedroom apartments
£87,000
Tel 01403 272230

GREENHITHE
'Worcester Park'
3 & 4 bedroom homes
£83,000-£118,000
Tel 01322 386974

Persimmon

stantly changing gears, or at the top of a hill which may become icy in winter? Do you like the facade? What about the houses around it – are they well maintained?

- Car parking – if there is no garage, will parking be a problem? Is there room to build a garage or create off-street parking? Are resident's parking permits required? If it is near a train or tube station will commuters park on the road, making it difficult for residents to find spaces?
- Garden size – while a large garden may sound wonderful, grass has to be mowed and flowerbeds tended. Will you have time to do this?
- Security – is there a burglar alarm or security light? Is the street well lit if you are arriving home late at night? This is especially important if you will be living alone
- Local industries – are there any big factories or a farm nearby that may emit loud noises or smells or smoke? What about a restaurant or pub which may cause noise late at night, and litter in the street?
- Amenities – is it near enough to local amenities such as shops, pubs or public transport?
- Roof – check the repair of the roof. Are there any tiles missing or loose? Does the chimney stack look in good condition? A pair of binoculars may be useful for scanning these areas. If it is a flat roof, check when it was laid and whether it has ever needed repair. Are gutters and drainpipes in good repair?

- Walls – are there any bulges or cracks in the outer walls which may be caused by the settlement of the foundations or by tree roots?
- Brickwork – what is the state of the pointing between the bricks, as cracks and gaps let in damp? Do the bricks themselves look in good condition?

INSIDE

- Entrance hall – is there an outer porch to protect against the weather? How wide is it – is there space to park prams, pushchairs or bicycles in it? What direction does the front door face and is it well lit?
- Sitting room(s) – are they big enough? Take a tape measure with you to make exact measurements, especially if it is an irregularly shaped room. Is the room light enough – are the windows big enough and in convenient places? How many plug sockets are there?
- Dining room – is it near enough to the kitchen? Is it big enough to fit your dining room suite in and still leave room to walk round it? Which way do windows face and is it light enough?
- Kitchen – if you have set your heart on a spacious kitchen, is it big enough? Are there enough work surfaces for your requirements? Count the number of power points – are there enough for all your equipment? What about cupboards and storage space? Which way does the window face and is the room well

100% PART EXCHANGE

ventilated? If the window faces south or west it may get too hot during the day. Could you keep an eye on a child in the garden from it? Where does the door lead out into, the hall, lounge or dining room? Is this convenient? Can you eat in the kitchen as well as cook if this is important?

- Utility room – if there is one, is it big enough to house a washing machine and tumble drier? Is there room to hang clothes out, both indoors and outside?
- Staircase – is it wide enough, well lit and not too steep for your purposes? Will young children or the elderly be able to get up it easily?
- Bedrooms – how many are there? Are they big enough to fit all your furniture in? Which way do they face? Do windows look on to a noisy road or brightly-lit street? Do they have fitted furniture and could they easily be converted into a nursery or study in the future?
- Bathroom(s) – are there enough of them? Is there a separate toilet either upstairs or downstairs? If you have elderly people or small children living in the house a downstairs cloakroom is often a good idea. Is the plumbing efficient and does everything work? Check where the water supply and waste pipes run in the building
- Other rooms – is there an extra room which could be used as a study, playroom, nursery or for storage? What about lofts and basements? Could they be converted into useful living space?

OTHER POINTS TO NOTE

There are some other key things to note when wandering round a property:

- What type of heating does it have and is the system in good repair? Check the boiler for rust spots which indicate leakage
- If the property has a loft, is it well insulated, and are tanks and pipes well lagged?
- How high are the ceilings? The higher they are the more costly the house will be to heat
- How well sound-proofed are the walls? This is especially important if you are looking at a terraced or semi-detached house or a flat or maisonette
- Are there any damp patches on walls or ceilings which could indicate leaks or rising damp?
- Are the hall and doorways large enough to get your furniture in? Is the flat itself big enough to accommodate all your possessions?
- Does the house appear structurally sound, with no unexplained sloping floors, ceilings or walls?
- Are you happy with the layout of the property? If it is open plan, will the lack of privacy annoy you?

You may think you have found the ideal house, but there are still a few points you should ask yourself:

How long has the property been on the market? If its been a long time, why is it difficult to sell? Will you be able to sell the house easily in the future? You may have decided that this is your last property, but circumstances can change. Always consider future selling problems when

buying. Will the property retain or even increase its value? Obviously, much depends on market conditions and a home is normally a long-term proposition. However, the investment side should never be ignored.

Try and talk to the current owners or tenants of the property about the house and area. Ask them about neighbours – they are legally obliged to tell you if they have ever formally complained to the police about them.

If you are satisfed that the house will not become a millstone in the future, you can listen to that inner voice. Do get a good feeling from the house and will you feel comfortable in it? A lot of people have a gut feeling about a house and feel immediately comfortable or uncomfortable. If it doesn't feel right immediately, it probably never will.

If after visiting the property several times you are sure it is the one for you, then it is time to make an offer.

REMEMBER ...

- Viewing more than one or two properties at the same time is likely to be confusing and counter-productive
- Aim to get an overview first – you can always go back and check the details
- Take a friend – not only is it safer, you will also have the benefit of an extra, objective, pair of eyes
- Take a notebook with you – this will help when you come to compare one property with another
- Visit the house at different times of the day, so you can check levels of noise and light
- Check all the rooms carefully – and don't forget the outside of the house
- Don't forget to look for signs of damp, make sure that the rooms are big enough for your furniture, that the layout of the house suits your requirements, and that there is adequate heating
- Trust your intuition, and use your imagination – a coat of paint can work wonders

FEES
SURVEY

4

BUYING – HOW IT WORKS

WHEN you've found a home you like, it's time to talk seriously to the estate agent who sent you details or showed you around the house for the first time.

An estate agent is a salesmen, whose job it is to value a home, put it on the market and then find a buyer. The majority of estate agents are members of professional bodies such as the Royal Institution of Chartered Surveyors, the Incorporated Society of Valuers and Auctioneers or the National Association of Estate Agents.

Bear in mind one very important point – he or she is the agent of the seller, not the buyer. In other words, he's on the seller's side, not yours. This means his job is to get the best price for the property. Agents are remunerated by getting a percentage of the agreed sale price but it is also their job to price houses realistically. The estate agent has to find buyers, a fact which can be utilised by the buyer with strong nerves.

The paperwork produced by agents has become much clearer in recent years. The reason is the 1991 Property Misdescriptions Act, which bans false or misleading statements of the kind which would waste hours of your time in getting you to view unsuitable properties. This sort of stuff is now illegal:

> a perceived sui [correct] generic residence of chalet design with a characteristic Tyrolean veranda facade is secreted within a secretive garden glade offering privacy without isolation. The liberated desideratum interior provides an emancipated environment in which the indigene may explore and experiment with furnishing creating a perpetual flux of mood.

It referred to a small semi-detached in Rochdale, Greater Manchester.

The Act also binds the person who is selling the house, whether he is selling privately or through an estate agent. The estate agent will have asked them specific questions about the property to produce reliable information for you and other prospective buyers. This covers claims about facilities and amenities. This is definitely to the buyer's advantage.

NEGOTIATING A PRICE

The basic question you need to ask is: is the asking price right? Or will you need to negotiate a price reduction? First of all, find out from the estate agent whether the seller will take an offer. They almost certainly will, as this will have been allowed for in the asking price. Typically, most sellers add 5–10 per cent to the price, which they are prepared to forgo. Do you want to knock them down further?

If you like a property, your own research in estate agents' windows and local newspapers should have given you some idea of how realistic the asking price is. You will be in a stronger bargaining position still if you can establish, through innocent questioning of the sellers, a number of key facts. You are looking for factors which put him under pressure to take a lower offer if he really wants a sale.

- Why are they trying to move? If they are in a hurry, they may be under tremendous pressure to cut their price for a quick sale. This could happen if they are moving their job to another part of the country, for example, or if a chain threatens to break down.
- How long has the property been on the market? A lengthy period usually means that the seller is asking far too much. It could mean that there is something wrong with the house, but it is more likely that the seller refuses to face reality. Many house owners still desperately want to believe that their home is worth as much today as it was in the runaway housing boom of the 1980s, which in many cases is just not true
- Have any offers already fallen through? For economic reasons, most people selling their house will stay with the same estate agent, so he should know the answer to this question. One common reason for a sale to fall through is a poor survey
- When did they buy? If the sellers bought a small property in the late 1980s, they may – particularly if they were first-time buyers – be in, or close to, negative equity (where the size of the outstanding mortgage is bigger than the actual value of the house or flat). If so, this will limit how far you can bargain them down
- Although the agent is acting for the seller, he should have a realistic view of his clients' expectations. If they

have put their house on the market at an unrealistic price, he may hint to you that this is the case

MAKING THE OFFER

You can make an offer through the agent, or direct to the seller. Some sellers want the agent to handle everything; others are quite happy to deal direct. There is a lot to be said for letting the agent handle the negotiations as they are experienced and can take a calm overview of the deal.

Do not be tempted to agree to suggestions that you deal with the seller direct in order to cut out the estate agent. Apart from anything else, the estate agent would still be able to claim his commission from the seller if he had introduced your business.

- Estate agents have a legal obligation to report offers to the client – even the silly ones. Irrespective of whether you put an offer through the estate agent, or make it direct to the buyer, don't immediately offer your top price. Give yourself a margin so that you have some space to move upwards. An undershoot of 10 per cent is a reasonable guideline
- If you feel that you are getting close to a deal, remember that negotiation works best when both sides feel that they have gained something, so don't try to extract the last penny: after all, the house-buying process in England and Wales gives people plenty of time to change their minds
- Make your offer 'subject to contract' – that way you are not committed if a survey reveals something nasty or,

as may happen, the person buying your house pulls out

- Once you make an offer which is accepted by the seller, some agents ask you to pay a small returnable deposit – £100 or so – as a token of good faith. There is little necessity for this and you would be entitled to refuse

FINDING A SOLICITOR

The next step is for you and the other side to exchange names and addresses of solicitors, who can start work behind the scenes.

If you haven't already got a solicitor, then finding one is often a matter of luck. A good lawyer is worth his weight in gold and is an investment for the future. A personal recommendation is always the best way to find a solicitor, but if this doesn't work your local Citizens' Advice Bureau will have a list. The estate agent will be able to recommend one too, but it's much better to find your own.

The building society also needs to check that its legal interests are looked after, but to save money, lenders are normally happy for your solicitor to do this too. The only exception is some one- practitioner firms, which are often not on building societies' approved lists.

An efficient and speedy solicitor can take a great deal of the strain out of the house-buying process. Unfortunately, however good your lawyer is, it can still seem to take an eternity to become the lawful owner of your new home.

Part of the problem is that your solicitor is himself in the hands of others. For progress to be made, he depends on others – council officials, the other side's lawyers – to return and fill in forms and provide crucial information on time.

You have no control at all over any of this, which is why buying and selling houses is so stressful. There's little you can do to speed matters up, but it's in your own interest to keep as calm and relaxed as possible. And don't keep on plaguing your solicitor for information. It could add to your costs and irritate your solicitor.

The lawyer's job is to arrange the legal transfer to you in such a way that you have total ownership over all of it and nobody else has any rights over it. This is called obtaining good title. It sounds simple enough, although the patchwork of land law has grown intricate over the centuries and is difficult to master for the layman, but for any good solicitor it is usually a mechanical process: bread and butter work.

LEGAL COSTS

Solicitors' fees add to the cost of house-buying, but in fact they have fallen in recent years as a result of competition. In any case, it is often the add-on costs which really push the cost of home-buying up, rather than solicitors' fees as such.

There are certain costs in the house-buying process which are unavoidable:

- Fees to register your ownership of the property at the Land Registry
- Stamp duty – a tax to the government of 1 per cent of the purchase price on any home valued at more than £60,000. You pay this on the entire price – not just the balance above £60,000
- Searches to discover if any planning applications will affect your property. All of these are on top of the solicitor's own professional fees

- VAT (Value Added Tax) of 17.5 per cent will be charged on some of these

There is no longer a solicitor's scale charge for handling your house purchase. Fees are usually based on a percentage of the house price. Ask what they are beforehand. Take a little time to shop around by telephone. Beware of legal friends who might offer to do the work for you on the cheap – all too frequently, it isn't any cheaper than using your local firm. There are also people around called licensed conveyancers, who usually charge less than solicitors for doing the same job. But home-buying is a fine opportunity to find yourself a solicitor, who may be able to help with other problems in the future.

This is what it cost to buy a £100,000 terraced home in north London in 1995. It is immediately clear that the actual solicitor's bill is not huge – it is the extras on top which put the price up:

Stamp duty (1 per cent of the purchase price)	£1,000.00
Land Registry fees	£230.00
Searches (done privately to speed up the process)	£112.79
Legal fees	£300.00
VAT	£52.50
TOTAL	£1,695.29

DIY CONVEYANCING

It might be tempting to try to save money by doing the legal work yourself. This is quite legal – but probably unwise, for the following reasons:

- Britain is an increasingly litigious society, and it is comforting to know a good lawyer. House-buying is the ideal time to find one
- Doing it yourself saves money but you have to spend your time on the job, and most of the work will need to be done during working hours
- Conveyancing is bread and butter work to a solicitor – but difficult technical work for you
- If you do it yourself, you can't blame anyone else if it goes wrong – or seek compensation from them

THE VALUATION

Once your mortgage application has been received by the building society or bank, your lender will then instruct a surveyor to have a good look at the property to discover whether it is worth the money the society will lend you. This is in case you cannot pay the loan and it has to repossess, but it also gives you some valuable professional guidance as to whether the house is worth the money you are going to borrow and pay interest on.

The surveyor is a professionally qualified individual, and is usually a member of either the Royal Institution of Chartered Surveyors or the Incorporated Society of Auctioneers and Valuers. He will be on the look-out for the kind of deep-seated horrors which you as a non-expert may well have missed when you visited.

They include serious structural problems such as subsidence or heave, damp, rising damp, wet or dry rot, defects with the roof and chimney, poor wiring, which can be very

dangerous, DIY work which needed building and/or planning consent, and problems with the drains. All of these can be expensive and troublesome to put right.

There are three types of surveyor's report:

- Valuation report – this will be required by and organised by your lender. It is for the lender's benefit primarily but the lender will almost always let you have a copy. It will cost around £125 for a £50,000 property. The report contains only the barest details, and is essentially confirmation that the house is worth what you are trying to borrow. Your home loan will be based on the property value according to this valuation report – which may be less than the asking price you have agreed with the seller. A valuation report is nothing like good enough to reveal any serious and expensive defects, yet, incredibly, more than nine out of ten home-buyers rely on it just the same. The fees for a valuation report are on a set scale: so, for example, the Halifax Building Society will charge £125 if the purchase price is less than £50,000, £165 if less than £100,000, £195 if less than £150,000, and so on

- Homebuyer's report – this goes into considerably more detail and probably runs to 10–12 pages. You can commission the same building society or bank surveyor to undertake this at the same time as he does the valuation report. It costs around £300 for the same £50,000 property and should tell you all that you realistically need to know about the property – for example, any defects or problems – and a lot more that you don't
- Full structural survey – this is often done by a structural engineer, commissioned by you. You are unlikely to need this unless you're buying a very old house to do up, or a special type of property, and need specialist guidance. It can sometimes be recommended if a home-buyer's report discovered serious defects. In practice, if that happens, you're usually better off finding another property

The lender will send you a copy of the detailed housebuyer's report or structural survey. Both are likely to be fairly worrying documents. Surveyors naturally write in the language of their profession and, to cover themselves, they point out all possible defects to the point where it may seem that your dream home is about to fall down. But don't worry unduly – the solution is to talk to the surveyor about any queries. He will probably be more forthcoming over the phone and put it all into perspective for you.

Even a depressing survey report can be useful ammunition for you. If the surveyor does discover serious defects and you still want to go ahead, it gives you a good way of getting the price reduced to compensate for the cost of the work which will need doing.

Really serious defects, however, may lead to the survey recommending a retention – that is, that the building society withholds part of the loan until the remedial work the surveyor recommends has been done to the required standard. Unless you have spare cash to cover this gap, you must either pull out or negotiate a bridging deal with the bank.

If you finally decide that the problems which have been revealed are too daunting or expensive for you to overcome, then pull out now – before you have made any serious commitment. You will lose your valuation/survey fee, but will have bought peace of mind.

A practice is growing among sellers to have their own survey done on the house, for which they will charge you a modest fee, before it comes on to the market. The advantage is that it cuts out the time required for a would-be buyer to obtain a survey – and takes away the shock of you finding something nasty in the woodwork later. However, the buyer will still need a valuation report at least.

Houses less than ten years old should be covered by the National House Builders' Council Guarantee Scheme. This protects you against faulty workmanship resulting from the building work not complying with the standards set down by the NHBC. For two years the builder is obliged to put things right, followed by an eight-year insurance period providing extra cover. There are benefits attached to such a guarantee, but it's not a reason for not having a proper survey done.

REMEMBER ...

- The estate agent is working for the seller and so has their interests at heart but, by the same token, they must find a buyer
- If you are going to try to negotiate, look for factors which could force the seller to take a lower price
- You can make your offer direct to the seller, or through an agent – the latter may help by providing you with a calm, objective overview of the deal
- Safeguard yourself by making the offer 'subject to contract'
- Avoid DIY conveyancing – legal costs are highly competitive now, and buying a house is a great opportunity to find a good solicitor who could prove very useful in the future
- A good survey will highlight any deep-seated structural problems. The surveyor will be able to put these in perspective for you, but don't be afraid to pull out if the problems seem insurmountable
- Last, but not least – be patient

5

EXCHANGING CONTRACTS

THE first legally binding step on the road to your new home is the exchange of contract with the seller. Before exchange you can still withdraw your offer. From the point of exchange onwards, the stress is off because you are both committed to the deal and you will be asked to put down a non-refundable deposit .

This is traditionally 10 per cent of the price but 5 per cent is often acceptable, particularly if you have indicated that you will need a 95 per cent mortgage. If you pull out after exchanging contracts you lose your deposit and may be sued for breach of contract.

Much legal work is needed when houses change hands. The reason is that the law demands that all contracts for the sale of land are set down in writing, which is not the case with other contracts of sale.

Yet, paradoxically, the law gives people buying homes very little protection. There is no guarantee of any kind that the house is in good shape, or even that the seller has any legal right to sell it at all! It is up to the buyer to satisfy himself on these points – hence the need for a solicitor.

- Good title – the solicitor will want to see hard evidence that the seller has what is called 'good title' to the property – in other words, that he genuinely owns the property and is in a position to sell it. The seller's solicitor will do this by providing either copies of the title deeds or a copy of the entry at the Land Registry. This is rock solid legal proof of ownership which is guaranteed by the state
- Others' rights – your solicitor will also want to be sure that no one else has any rights which could stop you getting full possession. Sitting tenants come into this category, as might a wife who is not the owner of the property – a potential problem if matrimonial difficulties are the reason for the sale. In practice, if a sitting tenant is discovered, you will almost certainly want your offer to be withdrawn
- Leasehold – your solicitor will check the detailed terms of the contract of sale provided by the seller's solicitor and, if the property is leasehold, he will also check the terms of the lease. While these tend to be fairly standard documents, he will check to make sure that there are no especially oppressive clauses lurking in the lease such as ones which limit what you can do with your property
- Rights of way – his next job is to check that no one else has any rights of way over the property, find out exactly where the boundaries are and where your responsibility for them lies. The title deeds will provide this information
- Restrictive covenants – another issue which will concern your solicitor is whether there are any restrictive

covenants which could limit what you can do with your new home

- New developments – the solicitor has to make sure that the local council is not planning anything nasty which will devalue your property – a new road by your back garden would fall into this category, for example. So he will send off a detailed list of queries – known as searches – to the town hall, while a different set goes to your local water company. This is standard procedure, but unfortunately, some local councils still take eternities to answer these, especially in inner London. As a result, many buyers choose to pay extra for a private search. This could cost around £70 plus. It often comes as an irritating surprise for financially stretched first-time buyers who sometimes find that these extra costs put a strain on their budgeting. But it saves time, and in the house-buying game, time saved means stress avoided

A tip here for the wise buyer: the answers to these searches show the direct impact on your property itself, not to the actual area where the property is situated. If there is derelict land nearby, a call to the council's planning department might reveal if the Home Office is planning to use it to build a new prison, for example. Once you are interested in an area, you should buy the local paper; such developments are always controversial and are likely to be heavily reported.

If you are buying a new home, there a number of special concerns which need to be tackled before the solicitor will be happy. He will want to be sure that the developer has agreed with the local council that roads will be built and that the council will then take over their maintenance. He will also want to be satisfied that the house will be properly built according to the specification with services laid on, and that the boundaries coincide with those laid down on the plan. A new development may contain restrictions about what homeowners can do with their property – your solicitor will check these and advise you about any especially onerous ones.

Finally, your solicitor will send the lawyer who is acting for the seller a document called 'enquiries before contract' which the seller's lawyer will discuss with his client, and send back. This has a standard list of queries about the property, most of which are of a technical nature. However, they are also designed to clarify a number of serious issues. One is the vexed question of exactly what the seller is leaving behind. Your own negotiations with the seller should have clarified this, yet disputes over so-called fixtures and fittings are one of the biggest sources of trouble. These enquiries give you a chance to get what you want set in stone. The general law is that everything that is a physical part of the house is included in the sale: these fixtures include plumbing installations and heating, as well as trees and shrubs.

However, moveable objects such as carpets, light bulbs, curtains, fridges, freezers and cookers, are classed as fittings. They therefore go with the seller unless you make specific arrangements to the contrary.

This leaves a wide category of objects on the borderline where disputes are depressingly common. They include bookshelves, curtain rails, bathroom fittings and TV aerials.

In practice, curtains and carpets are nearly always included in the price – they would be no use in the seller's new home as they will almost certainly not fit. But you should go

through room by room with the seller and agree clearly what is, and what is not, to remain. These pre-contract enquiries will also ask about what is becoming an increasingly important question – has the seller been in dispute with the neighbours? These questions must be answered honestly – not to do so can amount to a misrepresentation which may void the contract. Since noisy and disruptive neighbours are an increasing plague in Britain, this question – and its answer – is an important protection for you.

There is space on the form for any other questions, so if anything else is bothering you, ask the question and get it answered to your satisfaction. Remember that the general legal principle is that the seller does not have to volunteer information about the house, but if you ask for it, he has to answer truthfully.

When all this has been done, the solicitor should ask you to visit him to go through it all in detail. If you have any queries or questions or uncertainties, now is the time to raise them. Finally, if

- Local searches show nothing nasty being planned and you are happy with the replies to enquiries put to the seller
- A mortgage offer has been made in writing
- The surveyor has made a satisfactory report
- Your solicitor is happy about the legal side
- You have a deposit ready
- Both sides are agreed upon a completion date

you should then be in a position to exchange contracts. In England and Wales, this means that you are both committed to the sale. You can breathe at last.

GAZUMPING AND GAZUNDERING

Sadly, gazumping is returning on the back of a rising property market.

The problem is that in England and Wales, neither side is legally bound to the deal until contracts are actually exchanged. So at any time before then, either side can pull out. What this means in practice is that the seller who has accepted your offer is free to accept a higher one in the meantime. If he does, there is nothing you can do about it, even though you have paid money in surveyor's and legal fees.

It is often hard to know what to do in this situation. Offer more and you could easily start a spiral of offer and counter-offer with all the expense and insecurity that implies. Drop out, and you lose the money you have paid so far.

Estate agents are often blamed for encouraging gazumping, which is not entirely fair. In their defence they point out that they have a legal obligation to pass higher offers on to their client, and it is clients who then choose to accept them. They have a good point.

Conversely, the days of falling property prices saw unscrupulous buyers cut their offers just before exchange of contracts, putting the seller in a terrible situation. This was known as gazundering and was equally legal, if equally unethical.

Lawyers and politicians have been wrestling with this situation for years but so far to no avail. In England and Wales all you can do to protect yourself is to offer the seller a lock-out deal. Under this, the seller makes a legal agreement with you not to sell to anyone else in return for a fee (deductible from the eventual purchase price), on condition that contracts are exchanged within a set period. This is an excellent idea. The honest seller has nothing to fear, while you lose the fear of being gazumped. You do, however, stand to lose your fee if you pull out, perhaps because of a bad survey. Your solicitor will be able to explain the mechanics of this for you.

Contract races should be mentioned here too. Sometimes a seller with a nice house in a popular area will have so little difficulty in selling that he decides to offer the house to the first person to come with a contract. This is a situation which is prejudicial to your mental equilibrium – you face costs and stress and may still not win. Contract races are best avoided – especially as the seller is not in law bound to accept the first contract anyway! If someone mentions a contract race, find another property: there are always plenty to choose from.

EXCHANGE AND COMPLETION

This is a physical process – both sets of lawyers physically swap identical contracts, signed by both parties, although the actual moment of exchange is usually done over the phone using procedures laid down by the Law Society and accepted by all solicitors. From this moment on, you are committed to the deal. The contract will provide for stiff financial penalties if you do not complete as planned. The completion date will have been agreed by both parties and will form part of the contract. After exchange, your solicitor will prepare the transfer document which transfers the legal ownership to you.

The solicitor will make final checks aimed at showing undisclosed mortgages or disputes. On completion day, you can legally move in. The buyer pays the balance of the selling price through his lawyer, who will have been sent a cheque for this by the lender. The seller's deeds are handed over to the buyer's solicitor, who will pass them on to the mortgage lender as security for the loan. On this day, traditionally a Friday, the seller must move out and the keys are handed over to the buyer.

Normally, you must pick the keys up from the estate agent at completion. Sellers are reluctant to give them earlier just in case the purchase money does not arrive and you have already moved in.

After completion, the solicitor will advise the lender that completion has happened, inform the freeholder if applicable, register the change of ownership at the Land Registry, pay any stamp duty to the Inland Revenue, send the deeds to the building society and, last but not least, send you a completion statement and bill.

There is one point that is important for unmarried couples buying a property together: one cannot inherit from the other at all unless they have made a will. So both should make a will now. They should also have their solicitor register their ownership as 'joint tenants'. This means that if one person dies, the other automatically inherits their share of the house. It does not pass into the estate and so cannot be hit by inheritance tax.

IF SOMETHING GOES WRONG ...

Despite the stress and the agony, in the end, it usually works out. Sadly, there are a number of cases each year where this is not so, and getting redress can prove difficult. Here is where to complain about some of the more common problems:

- Lawyers overcharging – you can apply to the Law Society, the solicitors' professional body, for something called a remuneration certificate. This states whether the bill is fair and reasonable. Law Society – 113 Chancery Lane, London, 0171 242 1222
- Negligent solicitors – the Office for the Supervision of Solicitors (OSS), which is the renamed Solicitors Complaints Bureau, can consider complaints about poor service and conduct, but not negligence complaints where more than £1,000 is at stake. You must either sue or try to establish a claim before the Solicitors' Indemnity Fund, which insures solicitors.

Either way you need legal advice which is going to cost you. OSS – Victoria Court, Dormer Place, Leamington Spa, Warwickshire, CV32 5AE. There is a Legal Services Ombudsman which can review decisions of the OSS

- Negligent surveyors – a difficult one, this, because negligence in law is difficult to define. It does not mean that the surveyor made a mistake, but that the mistake was gross and one which a skilled professional ought not to have made. Proving this can be difficult. The Royal Institution of Chartered Surveyors does have an arbitration procedure, but this can only be used if the surveyor agrees to it. If he doesn't, you have to go to court. This is expensive and uncertain, and a recent legal decision reduced your rights if you do win. Speak to your solicitor first
- Estate agents – the big estate agency chains, but currently not most independents, support an ombudsman scheme. The ombudsman can look into rows over infringements of legal rights and unfair treatment, but not surveys. His latest report showed 2,707 enquiries which led to 266 adjudications, one client winning £5,000 compensation from an agent who had no case for claiming commission on a house sale. The Ombudsman for Corporate Estate Agents – Beckett House, Bridge Street, Salisbury, Wiltshire SP1 2LX

BUYING AT AUCTION

An auction is not always the place to find a bargain. Professional buyers and property developers generally ensure that the bidding for anything decent is competitive and an unsuspecting amateur should be wary of overbidding. However, you can often find unusual properties or repossessions at an auction which high street estate agents may find difficult to market. Here are the basic rules:

- Once the hammer falls, contracts are deemed to be exchanged and the property is yours. 10 per cent of the price is normally required immediately, with the balance 28 days later. You should make sure that all the necessary finance is in place
- You will have to do all the legal work, survey and searches before the auction. Some sellers provide all or part of this information up front, but costs will eventually be passed on to the buyer. If you do not buy the property, any expenses you have incurred will be lost
- Many properties are sold subject to a reserve. Agents generally give a guideline price which is often just above the reserve figure. Some auctions brochures may have the clause 'unless previously sold'. This means the seller is open to offers before the auction
- Do not get carried away during the bidding. Fix your price first and stick to it. If a property fails to meet its reserve it will be withdrawn. You can still negotiate with the auctioneers afterwards to see if the seller will accept a compromise price

REMEMBER ...

- Use local papers and the planning department of the local council to check future developments in the area which could affect the value of your property. A good solicitor will be looking out for these, too
- The law gives home buyers little protection. Your solicitor's expertise will be invaluable when it comes to checking on rights of way, good title and the existence of any restrictive covenants which could affect what you can do with your property
- Use your solicitor as a go-between to solidify your negotiations with the sellers. What exactly are they leaving behind? Have they had any disputes with the neighbours? If so, what happened and why?
- Until contracts are exchanged, you have no legal protection from gazumping or gazundering – but you can protect yourself with a 'lock-out' deal
- Avoid contract races – it's better (and less stressful) to look for another property
- Unmarried couples buying a house together should both make a will to ensure that the other will inherit the property

(*continued*)

- Make sure all your queries are answered to your satisfaction before you exchange – exchanging contracts is a legally binding commitment, and there are financial penalties for failing to complete
- Auctions can be a good place to find unusual properties or repossessions

6

SO YOU'VE EXCHANGED ...

CONGRATULATIONS! It may have taken many months to get to this stage and now you only have a short time to prepare for the move.The standard form of house purchase contract may contain a clause stipulating 28 days between exchange and completion, but this can be varied. At the time of exchange buyer and seller can agree a mutually convenient time to complete the deal: you don't have to wait for the full month if both sides want to complete earlier. Once you have exchanged and agreed a date, you have to give the buyer vacant possession on that day. If you do not, there will be financial penalties imposed on you. Make sure you are in a position to move.

- Chain gang – if you are in a chain of buyers and sellers, getting everyone to agree to a suitable date can be difficult. However, most people try to arrange everything on the same day to save the expense of a bridging loan or moving into temporary accommodation

BRIDGING LOANS

If you are buying your new home before you have sold your existing one, you will need to arrange a bridging loan. But they are not as easy to organise now as they were before the property market recession. Many of the big building societies – such as the Halifax – no longer make bridging loans.

Your best source is your bank. Most banks will make bridging loans, but stress that they don't have a 'package' product and it is very much a case of negotiating with your local bank manager. They will only make such a loan if they are confident about your ability to repay and you have a good record as a reliable customer.

Typically you might have to pay a fee of between £75 and £150 and you will then be charged interest of anything between 3 and 5 per cent over base rate on the amount you borrow. Bridging loans can either be open or closed. Open loans are when your property is still up for sale and no offer has been made, while a closed bridging loan is when you have exchanged but not yet completed. Normally charges on a closed bridging loan are quite a bit cheaper as the bank knows that you will be completing, whereas on an open loan it has no idea how long it will be before you will be able to sell your home and repay the money.

COUNTDOWN TO COMPLETING

The next few weeks are going to be some of the busiest of your life as you organise the practical side of moving:

- Insurance: you must take out insurance on the buildings from the date you exchange contracts. If you are buying a leasehold, you may find that the ground landlord already has this insurance in place – get your solicitor to enquire. If you are arranging a mortgage, the lender will in any case insist that the property is insured on exchange and may offer to do this for you. Until you move your belongings in, you will only need buildings insurance, not contents cover

- Removals: once you have fixed the moving date, you will need to book a removal firm. How much you will have to pay depends on many factors, including where you live. Those living in Greater London will face the highest charges. Someone moving 20 miles from a three-bedroom semi-detached house would pay an average of £412, acccording to a survey by the Woolwich Building Society in Greater London. This is exactly double the cost of a similar move in the north of England at £206. According to removal firms, moves of more than 150 miles would add more to the cost than difficult access for vehicles. However, both of these factors are more significant in cost terms than difficult access within the property, which in turn was more important than the need to move awkward pieces of furniture
- Get several quotations – you will be surprised at how much they differ
- The British Association of Removers can supply details of companies in your area
- Do not accept telephone quotations but make sure the estimator visits your property
- Decide on what level of service you want. This can

range from getting the removers to pack and unpack everything down to simply providing packing cases which you pack and unpack yourself

- Describe your new house to the estimator to make sure there are no unforeseen problems at the other end, such as difficult parking or restricted access
- Make sure your household contents policy will cover your possessions in transit – you may have to pay a small additional premium
- DIY move: this is the cheapest way to move – but also the most tiring. Major removal company Pickfords estimate that a third of a million people move every year without hiring a professional company. They have recently launched Selfmove, which provides specially

equipped vehicles with tail lifts and packing materials (0800 901010)

- Storing: if you are unable to move into your new property when you complete your sale, you will have to put your furniture into store. Yellow Pages can provide a list of suitable facilities or you can ask the British Association of Removers. There are generally three types of storage:
  (1) Space rented in a depository – normally, items are stored loose and you should be able to inspect them from time to time – there may be a charge for this
  (2) Containers – this method is becoming more popular and economical. Items are packed in containers at your house and stored unopened in a depository
  (3) Self store – you can rent space in a secure purpose-built warehouse and control the items yourself. Units come in different volume sizes which will decide the monthly rental

It is unlikely that your household policy will cover items in storage and some insurers are not prepared to take on this risk. However, the storage company will normally be able to arrange special cover but check out rates as such cover is usually quite expensive. Don't be tempted to skip cover, though – there have been incidents when depositories have burnt down and if you don't have insurance cover, you won't get any compensation. Make sure that you have sufficient cover for all your valuables and look at policy exclusions and excesses. Small valuables can be deposited at the bank but there will be a monthly or quarterly charge.

- You should keep an inventory of all the items in storage

- It is also a good idea to arrange ready access to items which you may need to withdraw earlier
- Find out how much notice you have to give to get your goods out, and make sure you know the charging period – often you have to pay for all or part of a month, and if you store goods for a month and two days you have to pay charges for two months

TAX BREAKS IF YOUR EMPLOYER ASKS YOU TO MOVE

If your employer helps you to move house any payments you receive, or any goods or services provided for you, are part of your taxable earnings, but if you relocate for job purposes, the first £8,000 of any help you receive is exempt from tax as long as certain conditions are met. You can qualify for this tax break if:

- You have to move home either to take up a new job with a new employer, or to take up a new job with your existing employer, or to continue your current job at a new location and
- Your existing home is not within reasonable daily travelling distance of your new workplace, and
- The home you move to is within reasonable daily travelling distance of your new workplace

You don't have to sell your existing home, but the home you move to must become your sole or main residence. If, for example, you only stay in your new home during the week, return to your family at your existing home most weekends, and there is no intention for your family to move permanently to your new home, your old home will probably remain your main residence. In that case you would not be entitled to the relocation exemption. But if you buy a new home, move into it with your family and rent out your old home, your new home will probably become your main residence.

There are certain time limits imposed.Your expenses must be incurred or the benefits provided before the end of the tax year following the tax year in which you start your new job. If, for example, you start your new job on 18 March 1996, you have until 5 April 1997 to use your exemption. However, if you don't use up all your exemption before the end of your time limit, your tax office may be able to arrange to extend the deadline.

The following expenses and benefits may qualify for exemption:

- costs of selling your existing home, whether you own it or rent it
- legal fees and services
- advertising
- disconnecting gas, electricity, water and telephone supplies
- loan redemption costs where the loan was secured or raised to buy your existing home
- rent, insurance, maintenance and security once the property is left empty and before you sell it
- costs of acquiring a new home including legal fees and services

- loan arrangement costs and mortgage indemnity premiums
- surveys, valuations, stamp duty and Land Registry fees
- connecting gas, electricity, water and telephone supplies
- cost of moving possessions
- travel and subsistence
- replacement domestic goods such as carpets, curtains and cookers
- interest payments on bridging loans

The main items that do not qualify for tax exemption include mortgage and housing subsidies if you move to a higher cost area, interest payments for the mortgage on your existing home, redirection of mail, council tax bills for your old home, purchase of uniforms for your children's new school, compensation for losses, such as having to give up a part-used season ticket, as well as compensation paid to you for any loss on the sale of your home.

If you are relocating to work in Britain from abroad, or moving to work abroad from the UK, any relocation assistance you receive may be taxable. If it is, you are entitled to the £8,000 exemption in the usual way.

PREPARING FOR THE MOVE

Any move will unearth large numbers of items which are no longer needed or which are unsuitable for your new home. Be ruthless – get rid of all unwanted goods. Here are a few suggestions:

- Place ads in the local paper – many cheaper items can be advertised free of charge and, even if you have to pay a small charge, it is likely to be well worthwhile so doing
- Sell more valuable pieces at auction or to a reputable antique dealer. Don't accept the first price you are offered and talk to several sources before you agree a deal – you will be surprised at how large a difference there is between different quotes
- Hold a garage sale – weekends are the best time – and make sure you advertise the sale so you get a good attendance
- Organise a stall at a car boot sale. Check local papers for ads on forthcoming sales and turn up early so you can organise the items you want to sell in an attractive way
- Try second-hand shops. You are not likely to be offered much of a price but it can be an easy and convenient way of getting rid of unwanted furniture, as they will usually come to your home and pick up the goods
- Get a quote from a house clearance dealer – but expect very little
- Local charities or jumble sales will often collect unwanted items. Although you won't get any money for it, you can feel at least it is doing someone some good
- Hire a skip for the rubbish – you will need a permit if it is parked on the road, and you will have to organise special flashing lights. Check with your local council before you order the skip

- Local councils have rubbish dumps and some provide collection services. Free skips are often placed in some strategic areas

CHANGE OF ADDRESS CARDS

Order these well in advance. Some removal firms will provide them free of charge if you give them your business. Royal Mail also provide free cards if you use their redirection service (see below). Otherwise, specialist printing shops should be able to print moving cards for you within a couple of days at reasonable rates.

PAYING YOUR BILLS

Apart from settling the local bills such as the milk and the papers, you will have to pay the utilities – gas, electricity and water – and the council tax up to the day you complete the sale.

- Council tax – write to your local council quoting your council tax reference. The rating year normally runs from 1 April to 31 March. If you move out on 1 June, you will be responsible for the tax due in April and May; that is, 61 days out of the 365. The local council will automatically work this out for you
- Water charges – these will be apportioned by the relevant water authority. Let them know the completion date and they will work out the final bill, taking into account the consumption if you are metered
- Gas and electricity – arrange to have the meters read on the day you leave. Most suppliers only need a few

days' notice and some will take your own reading over the telephone. Keep a note of the readings to check against your final bill. If you are moving to a new house, the builder is generally responsible for arranging installation. You will have to fill in application forms for the relevant supplier. If the property you are moving to is already occupied, the previous owner should arrange for meters to be read. However, this does not always happen, so it is often better to have them read on arrival. In any case take a note of the readings to compare with your first bill. If you are moving to a new supplier's area, you will normally have to fill in a fresh application form. Deposits are not required if you have been a prompt payer in the past

- Heating and lighting – you should not remove lamp holders or sockets or leave bare wires. Take extra light bulbs to the new property
- In winter it is good manners to ask the incoming buyer if the heating should be left on
- Make sure you know how the heating system in the new property works. Get details of the last service and any maintenance contract
- Washing machine and dishwasher – make sure you know how to disconnect the fill taps at the back of the machines. Drain off any remaining water
- Fridge – automatic defrost fridges will only need a wipe around. Others will need to be defrosted a day or two before the move
- Freezer – you can move a freezer without emptying it,

although it should not be completely full. Run the freezer on 'high' for a few days before the move. Both fridges and freezers can get airlocks in the cooling system, so make sure they are carried the right way up

- Telephone – a vital piece of equipment in any house move. Liaise with both your buyer and seller to make sure existing lines remain in use and that there are no unnecessary disconnection and reconnection charges. Ring 150 between 8am and 6pm Monday to Saturday, giving British Telecom the date when you want charges to stop. Make sure you have your customer account number handy. Let them know if your buyer wants to take over the number and the 'phone if it is rented. The rental charges will be apportioned on your next bill
- If you own your own 'phone, make sure there are suitable modern plug-in sockets at the new property and take the 'phone with you. If not, make sure you contact BT well in advance and organise the installation of the modern sockets as soon as possible after you have moved in
- If you move within the same telephone area, you can generally take your existing number with you, although there will be an extra charge
- If you need a new telephone line, arrange this as soon as possible by ringing 150. If there is a working line in the new property, and you take it over on the same day the previous occupant leaves, there is no connection charge
- Redirecting mail – the Royal Mail will redirect your

letters to your new address. Everything is sent first class in a separate package and they need one week's notice to be up and running. In the UK charges are £6 for one month, £13 for three months and £30 for one year. A separate fee is required for each different surname. A redirection form can be picked up at the Post Office or you can call 0345 777 888, using your credit card. Parcels can be redirected by calling Parcelforce on 0800 224466

Apart from the services we have already mentioned, there will be numerous people who should know about your move:

- Motor car – you will need to tell your car insurance company as your new property may be in a different risk area which could affect future premiums. In addition, you should inform the DVLC at Swansea, SA99 1BN, for both vehicle registration and driving licence. Don't forget the AA, RAC or other motoring organisation
- Bank account – you may want to transfer your account, although this is best left until after the move is complete. An extensive branch network, plus cash machines, means that long-range banking is very feasible. Also inform credit and charge card companies
- Other finance – this could include the registrars if you hold shares or unit trusts, your stockbroker and the building society. If you hold Premium Savings Bonds, send the holder's card to their office in Lytham St Annes, Lancashire FY0 1YN. National Savings Certificates and SAYE are dealt with at the Savings Certificate and SAYE Office, Durham DH99 1NS. Don't forget the taxman as well

Best
REMOVALS

- National insurance – write to your social security office quoting your NI number, if you receive benefits or pension
- Insurance – this not only includes life insurance policies but also insurance on your property. Don't forget to tell your broker
- Medical – the list can include your doctor – which you may need to change – dentist and private health insurers, as well as the hospital if you are receiving treatment
- Employer – tell your employer and make sure that the company pension fund is informed as well, if you are a member. Don't forget your professional association or trade union
- Social – this list can be enormous and includes friends, relatives, schools, charities, clubs, football pools, mail order, library, TV rental and TV licence
- Keys – last, and by no means least, make sure you have access to your new home. Arrange with the seller to pick up the keys on completion day

REMEMBER ...

- Make sure you give the buyer vacant possession on the agreed date, or you could incur financial penalties
- As soon as you have completed the legal side of the deal, you will need to arrange insurance, removals and storage
- Use the move as an opportunity to get rid of unwanted items – there are a number of ways, from auctions to car boot sales
- Remember to pay the bills at your old home and arrange with the utilities companies to take over the bills at the new one
- Liaise with your buyer and seller regarding telephones to avoid any unnecessary disconnection and reconnection charges
- Arrange with Royal Mail to have your mail redirected and have some change of address cards prepared – it may help to compile a checklist of all the people who will need your new address, whether for business or personal reasons
- If you are moving because of a job relocation, don't forget that the first £8000 of the costs incurred may be tax deductible

RAINY DAY
LIGHT
HEAT

7

CAN YOU AFFORD A MORTGAGE?

SOME people may be in the fortunate position of not having to borrow money to buy their homes, but the vast majority of first-time buyers and many families moving up the housing ladder to a more expensive home will almost certainly need to come to grips with the mortgage market.

Housing finance has changed dramatically in the last 15 years. Until the mid-1980s, mortgages were difficult to obtain and most people had to show evidence of regular saving with the building society in order to obtain a place in the mortgage queue. Apart from a few council loans, building societies were virtually the only source of mortgage funds. As interest rates were fixed by the societies' trade body, the Building Societies Association, there was little point in shopping around for a better deal.

This has all changed. Today's house-buyer has never had it so good. There is a wide choice of mortgage lenders, a huge range of mortgage products to suit different needs, interest rates are low and there are plenty of funds available for anyone who can show that they are able to keep up the monthly mortgage payments.

THE LENDERS

- Building societies – building societies are still the traditional starting point for most hopeful borrowers. They are seen to be more user-friendly than other lending organisations, and many would-be borrowers welcome the face-to-face contact they provide. Despite mergers and the well-publicised conversions of leading building societies into banks, there are still some 80 active building societies. These range from the giants, which have a branch in every major town and city, down to

small local operations which are geared to serving their own community. Building societies obtain their finances from the savers who invest with them. There are usually some six savers to every one borrower, and the managers have to balance the interests of the savers, who want the highest possible savings rates, with the borrowers, who want the cheapest possible mortgage rate. In recent years, societies have been able to borrow money on the wholesale money markets (where financial institutions lend money to each other), which has enabled them to be more flexible in the types of loans they can offer

- Banks – the High Street banks entered the mortgage market in a rather tentative fashion in the early 1980s. Now they are a major force and account for around half the entire number of new mortgages. The service they offer is, in many ways, identical to that of the building societies with whom they are competing for borrowers. The difference is that they are not as constrained by the interests of savers as building societies are, which is one reason why, for example, they can offer long-term fixed interest rates. But on the whole, their mortgage rates are in the same range as the building societies
- Centralised lenders – these are mainly organisations the public has rarely heard of. They tend to be specialist subsidiaries of major international banks and some British ones, which obtain their mortgage funds exclusively from the wholesale money markets. This is their strength and also their weakness: although the better centralised lenders will have standard

mortgage rates broadly in line with the big lenders, others will have the mortgage interest rates which are either cheaper or notably more expensive (as they now have been for several years) than those of traditional lenders. Centralised lenders sprang up in the housing boom of the 1980s and sold most of their loans through independent financial advisers and mortgage brokers and offer a range of different types of loans. They cater for people in search of special mortgage deals, including the self-employed. Centralised lenders had the reputation of lending money to just about anybody in the 1980s and, as a result, many are still saddled with bad debt problems. Borrowers with centralised lenders who are in arrears or have negative equity and so unable to move to a new lender have been charged a higher than average mortgage rate

- Telephone lenders – the last few years have seen an explosion of banks, building societies and insurance companies setting up companies to provide mortgages over the telephone. These companies offer slightly cheaper than average standard variable mortgage rates – since they have no expensive branch networks, they can pass on the saving as lower mortgage rates. These lenders are notorious for 'cherry picking' their customers. They can be very choosy about who they are prepared to lend money to

- Secondary lenders – these are recognised lending institutions, often subsidiaries of major financial groups such as banks, which specialise in lending money to men and women with poor credit records. People with county court judgments, records of arrears and other problems can often get mortgages from these companies. The companies are taking a risk on lending – and this is reflected in the price, which is often very high. Typically, interest rates are pegged 2 or even 3 per cent above the average rate

WHAT YOU NEED TO GET A MORTGAGE

No one has a right to a mortgage and lenders cannot be forced to lend money to people they do not trust to be able to pay off the loan. It is generally agreed that there was a lot of irresponsible lending on the part of building societies and banks in the housing boom of the late 1980s. Since the housing crash of the early 1990s, which left many people in arrears, lenders have become far more careful in deciding whether to grant a mortgage or not.

Whichever lender you go to, you will have to provide evidence that you will be able to keep up the mortgage payments on a loan, which typically will run for 25 years. These are the key documents your lender will require:

- An unbroken employment record for at least the last two years – your own word may not be sufficient. Most lenders will want to see a letter on headed notepaper from your boss saying how long you have worked with the company. If you have been with your present employer for less than two years, you will have to provide a reference from your previous company
- Proof of earnings – your pay slips may be sufficient,

but many lenders will want confirmation from your company's personnel department

- Proof of residency for two years – if you have been previously living in rented accommodation, your landlord will be asked to confirm this

- References from current and former landlords to cover the last two years – these need to show that you have paid the rent punctually

- Bank statements – you will be asked for copies for particular months over the last two to five years to provide additional evidence that the rent has always been paid promptly

- Bank reference – needed to show that you have been a responsible client accustomed to managing your personal finances properly

- Monthly outgoings – you will be asked to provide a list of all current outgoings against income showing rent, bills, council tax, credit card payments and any other significant monthly outgoings

- Certified accounts – the self-employed will need to supply these for at least three years. See below, where we look in detail at the position of the self-employed and contract workers

On top of this lenders will carry out a credit check with one of the many credit reference agencies in operation. This will list any former mortgage debts, and county court judgments. The golden rule is, tell the truth. Lenders will find out anyway. It is far better to tell the lender first and then make a case for being lent to.

If there is something on your file which leads the lender to turn down your loan application the lender does not have to explain why. However, he is obliged to tell you if any credit reference agency has checked your details. If you wish to query what is on your record you should obtain a copy of the agency's records on you and, if it is incorrect, get it amended. It costs £1 to obtain a copy of your record. The addresses of the two main credit reference agencies are:

CCN Group
Consumer Help Service
PO Box 40
Nottingham NG7 2SS

Equifax Europe UK Ltd
Department 1E
PO Box 3001
Glasgow G81 2DT

WORKING OUT THE COSTS

Whichever type of mortgage you ultimately decide to take (see Chapter 8), you want the best deal you can afford. There are several factors which will influence your ability to secure the best arrangement possible:

- Loan to value – this is jargon which might initially confuse new borrowers. This simply compares the value of the home you want to buy with the size of the mortgage you want to take out

- Deposit – the more you can put down towards the cost of your home, the greater the chance of reducing your costs. It is is possible to borrow 100 per cent of the price of your home (as agreed by the lender's valuers – not necessarily the same as the asking price). But the majority of lenders will prefer a deposit of at least 5 per cent of the value of the property. But it will be to your advantage to save up for a bigger deposit than this. Major lenders charge a lower interest rate if you are borrowing a smaller proportion of the value of the property. Special discounted rates can begin with a 10 per cent deposit, and with deposits of 25 per cent and more, the discounts look attractive.
- Mortgage indemnity guarantee – known as MIG, this is, in effect, a penalty imposed on borrowers with little or no deposit. Borrowers with deposits of less than 25 per cent (even if they are getting the discounted rate mentioned above) will usually have to pay this form of insurance.

There is a lot of confusion about MIG. Although it is the borrower who has to pay it, the benefit belongs to the lender. The borrower makes a one-off payment that covers the lender should the borrower be unable to pay off all the loan and the house has to be repossessed – and its value then is less than the mortgage outstanding. The difference between the two amounts is paid by the insurance company to the lender. If the borrower's circumstances improve, then the insurance company is within its rights to pursue him for the money it paid to the lender.

The cost of the MIG can be added on to the total value of the loan. It is not cheap, but the rates go down the larger your deposit is. There is no fixed scale, but these are typical MIG costs from a lender, Abbey National:

MIG costs on a house valued at £50,000 for mortgage lending

Deposit	MIG	Deposit	MIG
nil	£1,250	15%	£300
5%	£775	20%	£100
10%	£487	25%	nil

Some lenders will grant mortgages to people with no deposits. But as the figures above show, not only is there likely to be a higher interest rate, but there will also be a hefty MIG insurance premium to boot. Borrowers in this position may want to think twice. Not only are there these extra costs, but there are also other expenses such as removals, solicitor's and surveyor's fees, which could add another £1,000 at least to their immediate outgoings.

- Income multiple – lenders will usually advance you a sum of money which is related to the size of your earnings. The traditional amount is to lend three times the first salary and one times the second salary. However, variations are possible. For example, in households where both partners have good jobs with rising salary expectations, then a loan of two times each salary could be considered. If you have rising salary expectations, the three times earnings limits might be extended to as much as four times

SELF-EMPLOYED AND CONTRACT WORKERS

Lenders have always been shy of granting mortgages to the

self-employed and people working on fixed-term contracts. Lenders think there is a greater risk of unemployment or wage cuts meaning the mortgage won't be paid. However, over the last decade the numbers have been swelling and lenders can no longer ignore them. As a result it is now easier for contract workers and the self-employed to get mortgages, but there are still big hurdles in the way.

On top of the usual credit checks, lenders will usually want to see:

- Three years' accounts – a minimum of three years' worth of certified business accounts from a self-employed home owner are required to make sure there is a history of regular income going into the firm. Certified accounts have to be supplied by the trader's or firm's accountants
- Business checks – some lenders will also make enquiries to confirm that the business is viable and that it can count on future orders coming in
- Contract renewal – fixed-term contract workers also have to demonstrate that their contracts have been renewed a set number of times. They must also show that there is every likelihood that the contract will be renewed again in the future
- Employer's reference – this is to satisfy a lender that a contract worker's employment will probably continue

SELF-CERTIFICATION AND NON-STATUS LOANS

The self-employed have another route. Self-certification or non-status loans are popular with self-employed people who might, for example, keep their incomes low for business reasons or do not have enough years of business accounts to satisfy an ordinary lenders' loan requirements.

A self-certification mortgage is exactly what it says: basically, it lets a borrower say he can afford to pay the mortgage without having to show the ability to do so. This is not as strange as it sounds. Efficient accountants will use every tax break available to reduce self-employed and small business people's tax bills. The upshot of this is that their incomes may look far lower than they really are. Self-certification loans are a way around this problem. Self-employed people without three years of business accounts can also get these mortgages if they can show the potential for future earnings.

Self-certification loans are not cheap, and are commonly supplied by non-mainstream lenders whose base mortgage rate may be higher than usual. Borrowers will probably have to pay a slightly higher than average interest rate and will usually be asked for a deposit of at least 20 per cent. It is always worth trying to obtain a conventional mortgage with a traditional lender first. They may be prepared to be flexible about how much they will lend – four times income instead of the usual three times, for example – if there is a very good chance your income will grow over the next couple of years. A reputable mortgage broker (see page 125) should be able to help you find the best deal.

BAD DEBTS

The recession of the early 1990s is still taking its toll. Last year a massive 1.3 million county court judgments (CCJ)

were issued for non-payment of debts, and a further 350,000 mortgage holders are more than three months behind with their payments. If you manage to repay a debt within a month of the CCJ, it will be expunged from your record. But if you wait longer than a month to repay it, the CCJ will stay on your record for six years and appear on all credit checks.

Even if your circumstances are now stable, you will find it difficult to obtain a mortgage. However, some major lenders are willing to give people in this position a mortgage although they are very cautious about it. The CCJs must have been paid off and, if switching your mortgage, the arrears must have been for less than two or three months and must now be paid off. Secondary lenders are willing to give loans to people shut out of the mortgage market by CCJs. But these loans are very expensive, often 3–4 per cent higher than normal mortgage rates.

NEGATIVE EQUITY

The housing slump of the late 1980s and early 1990s introduced a new problem that is still with us – negative equity. This means that the value of a property has fallen so far that it is worth less than the mortgage paying for it. The borrower is therefore trapped in the property as they cannot sell it for enough to pay off the loan. This has hit people who put down very small deposits or no deposit at all, and also live in what are now unattractive starter homes, such as right-to-buy council flats, studio flats and converted flats. At its height in 1992 some 2.1 million homes were

blighted with negative equity. But it is still with us. At the end of 1996, it was estimated that some 400,000 were still weighed down with an average shortfall of £4,000 on the value of their homes.

It is possible to escape negative equity. The first and most obvious route is to pay off as much of the home loan as possible. The object is to reduce the value of the mortgage to the value of the property and then sell it without being saddled with an outstanding debt to the lender.

A number of lenders offer negative equity mortgages that lend up to 125 per cent of the value of a new property so that home owners can move to a new home taking the outstanding negative equity with them. Lenders which offer negative equity loans are likely to charge an extra slice of interest, usually on any money lent over 90 per cent of the new property, so check this out carefully.

SHARED OWNERSHIP

Low income working households can get on to the housing ladder using a housing association shared ownership scheme. Housing associations – non-profit-making bodies that provide low-cost social housing – let tenants buy a percentage of a property (usually 25, 50 or 75 per cent) and rent the rest. As and when they can afford to, the home owners can buy the rest of the home. These schemes are not available to everybody. Your income must be below the national average earnings of £17,500 a year, and there is usually a long waiting list.

A variation of this is Do-it-yourself shared ownership (DIYSO). DIYSO schemes let potential home owners find their own home on the open market. The house has to be worth less than a certain limit set by the association. It then buys the property and then sells it to the tenant on a shared ownership basis.

Lenders are often cautious about lending on shared ownership schemes and will only lend if there is a mortgage protection clause in place that acts in a similar way to MIG insurance, covering the lender if the house has to be sold for less than the value of the mortgage.

Your local authority's housing officer will be able to put you in touch with associations in your area. The National Housing Federation (0171 278 6571) will also provide useful information.

USING A MORTGAGE BROKER

There are so many different types of lenders and mortgages that you might wish to use the services of a mortgage broker. Certainly anyone whose circumstances fall outside the norm, either in terms of their own status or the type of property they are buying, could save a lot of time, effort and money by employing a mortgage expert.

A mortgage broker will have an up-to-date list of all the mortgage deals and interest rates currently on the market. In addition he will probably also have special relationships with several major lenders which will give him priority access to any special deals that come up.

Typically, you will have to pay a fee of £200–£300 for the advice, unless you are arranging life assurance, as part of an

endowment mortgage for example, through the mortgage broker. In that case, he will take the commission as payment. The leading mortgage brokers are independent financial advisers, not linked to any one insurance company or lender.

IF THINGS GO WRONG

In the event of problems arising with your mortgage either as a result of your lender's or your adviser's actions, you need to make sure that there is an official complaints mechanism for dealing with your grievance. There is a code of conduct governing the selling of mortgages to which banks and building societies adhere. If you feel that your lender has not fully informed you of the nature of the mortgage you have taken out, you should in the first instance take it up with the lender's own disputes procedure.

In addition there are the banking and building society ombudsmen schemes. These schemes will look at disputes between lenders and borrowers and decide who, if anyone, was at fault and award compensation – up to a maximum of £100,000 – if the complaint warrants it. The decision of each ombudsman is binding. Complaints about mortgage interest rates, however, are outside their terms of reference.

REMEMBER ...

- Shop around for your mortgage – it's a buyer's market
- You must be able to prove you will be able to keep up repayments, usually for a 25-year period. Conditions are even more stringent for the self-employed and contract workers
- Lenders will carry out a credit check, so don't be tempted to lie!
- Saving up for a substantial deposit could make you eligible for favourable discounts and help you to avoid the mortgage indemnity guarantee
- Self-employed and contract workers in particular may find a mortgage broker useful – but they can save time and money for anyone who wants to borrow
- Shared ownership can make buying a more economical proposition

8

DIFFERENT TYPES OF MORTGAGES

SOME two-thirds of homeowners have standard variable rate mortgages. This is the floating rate lenders charge that is in turn dictated by the bank base rate set by the Bank of England. The rate can move both up and down, so borrowers in this position do well when rates fall, but badly when they rise. Many big lenders have an annual review scheme for borrowers on their standard rates. At the end of each year the lender works out the average standard rate over the last year and borrowers then pay that rate. At the end of the year the average interest rate is recalculated and payments reset.

DISCOUNTED RATE MORTGAGES

These are standard variable rate mortgages with a percentage knocked off them for a set period. Lenders will take 1, 2 or 3 per cent off their standard rate for two or three years. The borrower then pays that rate. It can go up or down, but it will always be that set amount less than the standard rate.

Borrowers taking on these deals should beware of early redemption penalties. Often these last longer than the deals themselves. Borrowers wanting to move to a new lender within a set period must pay a penalty to their old lender – typically six months' gross interest or 5 per cent of the value of the loan. This adds up to over £1,800 on a £50,000 mortgage.

FIXED RATE MORTGAGES

These loans lock borrowers into a fixed interest rate for a set number of years – as little as six months or as many as 25 years. During this time the interest rate is guaranteed not to change. Locking into these rates gives comfort in knowing exactly what the payments will be for a while. But they are also a gamble in that borrowers are betting what interest rates will do over that time. Borrowers are betting interest rates will rise, so they will save money. This does not always happen and many borrowers have been stuck with 10 or 11 per cent rates while the standard variable rate was under 7 per cent. These deals also have early redemption penalties every bit as harsh as the ones on discounted rate loans and they can also last beyond the life of this mortgage.

CAPPED RATE MORTGAGES

These are another variation on the standard variable rate loan. In this case borrowers are guaranteed that the mortgage

interest rate will not go above a set level – the cap. While it is under the cap it can go up and down depending on what the standard variable rate is at the time. They give a combination of the best features of a fixed rate loan – certainty – and of a discounted rate loan – the rates can go down. Once again, the capped rate loans on offer have early redemption penalties.

CASHBACKS

The name is pretty self-explanatory. Borrowers take out a loan and the lender will then give the borrower a lump sum in return. Usually this is not more than 6 per cent of the value of the mortgage. These are a feature of standard as well as discounted and fixed rate loans, where they are often part of the deal. If a cashback is linked to a discounted or fixed rate loan, the rate paid on the mortgage will not be as good as it would be without the cashback. They also have early redemption penalties. Often borrowers have to repay the value of the cashback if they move lenders within five years.

HOW YOUR MORTGAGE WORKS

A mortgage is simply a long-term loan. A sum of money is borrowed and, until all the money is repaid, interest has to be paid on the outstanding balance owed. Over a typical 25-year mortgage period, the overall cost is between two and three times the original home loan. However, for many people the original value of their home is likely to be considerably higher.

The choice prospective home owners have to make is how to repay that loan. There are a number of routes borrowers can go down, each with their own particular pros and cons. But there are only two basic types of mortgages: repayment and interest-only.

Repayment mortgages

The repayment is the original type of home loan. As its name suggests, from the start you begin to repay some of the capital you have borrowed. However, to keep things simple for their mortgage customers, lenders devise a monthly repayment programme which, were interest rates to remain unchanged, would remain the same for the life of the loan. At first only a small amount of the monthly payments is used to repay capital; a far greater amount goes on interest payments. But over the years, the balance changes as more money is paid off, so the amount of interest due gets smaller. In turn this allows more money to go towards paying off the capital sum. By the end of the mortgage term the entire loan will be paid off.

How a repayment loan is paid off over 25 years

£50,000 loan assuming a 7.25 per cent interest rate with 15 per cent tax relief on the first £30,000 of the loan

Year	Net payment a month £	Interest repaid each month £	Capital repaid each month £	Debt at year end £
1	338.46	274.90	63.55	49,237.40
2	338.46	270.29	68.16	48,419.52
3	338.46	265.35	73.10	47,542.34
4	338.46	260.05	78.40	46,601.57
5	338.46	254.36	84.08	45,592.58
6	338.46	248.27	90.18	44,510.45
7	338.46	241.73	96.72	43,349.86
8	338.46	234.72	103.73	42,105.13
9	338.46	227.20	111.25	40,770.16
10	338.46	219.13	119.31	39,338.40
11	338.46	210.48	127.96	37,802.84
12	338.46	201.20	137.24	36,155.95
13	338.46	191.25	147.19	34,389.67
14	338.46	180.58	157.86	32,495.32
15	338.46	169.14	169.31	30,463.64
16	338.46	156.86	181.58	28,284.66

17	340.01	145.25	194.75	25,947.70
18	342.13	133.25	208.87	23,441.31
19	344.40	120.38	224.01	20,753.21
20	346.83	106.58	240.25	17,870.22
21	349.45	91.77	257.67	14,778.22
22	352.25	75.89	276.35	11,462.04
23	355.25	58.86	296.38	7,905.45
24	358.47	40.60	317.87	4,091.00
25	361.93	21.01	340.92	0.00

Source: *Halifax*

The advantages of a repayment mortgage are:

- Borrowers know that, provided they meet their monthly payments, the loan will be paid off at the end of the mortgage term
- Negative equity – where the mortgage is worth more than the house – is less likely to be a problem as the size of the loan is being reduced all the time, cutting the amount of negative equity
- Equity build-up – borrowers have to repay the loan when they move, but will often have built up a sizeable profit to put towards their next home
- Flexible – a repayment loan can be paid off in full at any time, lump sum payments can be made towards it, the mortage term can be shortened or increased at will and repayments can be made at intervals more frequent than once a month
- Repayments are not linked to stock market performance – so borrowers will never be caught out by a poor investment performance

But there are drawbacks too:

- No built-in life cover – borrowers need to take out separate life insurance to repay the mortgage should they die prematurely
- Early repayment options reduced – since none of the money is invested in stocks and shares there is no chance of an extra windfall payout if the stock markets do well

Interest-only mortgages

With an interest-only mortgage the borrower only pays the interest due on the loan, not the capital sum. At the end of the loan's life the borrower is expected to have saved up enough money elsewhere to pay off the loan. Although it is possible to take an interest-only loan where the society or bank doesn't wish to know anything about how you propose to repay it, in the great majority of cases, your lender will insist on knowing – and agreeing – your repayment proposals. In many cases, particularly where endowments are concerned, it will arrange the repayment vehicle for you. Historically these were known as endowment mortgages because they were linked to an endowment policy which would ultimately repay the loan. In recent years, however, other investment vehicles, such as personal equity plans and pension plans, have come to the fore as suitable ways of saving to pay off a mortgage as well. As only the interest element is paid off, these mortgages look cheaper than a repayment mortgage. To be strictly comparable you must include the cost of the savings vehicle which will provide

the capital lump sum actually to repay the loan at the end of the mortgage term.

Borrowers do not have to be locked into one type of mortgage repayment plan. It is possible to combine them, with different parts of the loans being paid off in different ways.

Endowments

Over half of the mortgages currently being sold will be paid off by an endowment policy. These are basically savings plans run by life insurance companies that incorporate life insurance. The money is paid in and invested on the stock market and, by the end of the term, enough capital should have built up to pay off the mortgage.

Insurance companies will work out how much needs to be paid into an endowment to pay the loan off, usually 25 years later. To cover the danger of a shortfall, they usually say that 80 per cent of the endowment payout should be enough to pay off the loan. This means that if bad performance hits returns, up to one-fifth of the expected value of the payout can be lost before there is any danger of a shortfall.

There are two main types of endowments. 'With-profits' is the name given to a kind of policy which guarantees that the amount earned on your investment at end of each year will not fall. Each year insurance companies pay a bonus which, once given, cannot be taken away. The price of these guarantees is that the investment performance of an endowment may not be sky-high, but the money is safe.

Unit-linked endowments directly reflect the performance of the underlying investments the insurance company has bought with your money (unlike with-profits funds, where there is a smoothing out process to cushion investors against bad years). When stock markets are rising, unit-linked policies should perform well, but if stock markets fall there could be a serious problem.

The advantages of using an endowment policy to back your mortgage are:

- Automatic life insurance cover – you do not need to shop around to find a suitable policy, and your mortgage will be repaid should you die prematurely
- Long-term good performance – for those who have stuck with the same policy for 25 years, endowment policies have been a rewarding investment. In many

cases, the policy has not only repaid the mortgage but given the policy-holder a tax-free lump sum on top

- Early repayment – with a unit-linked policy in particular, if stock market performance is good, there is a chance of either paying off the loan early or receiving an extra lump sum at the end of the term

The drawbacks of endowment policies are:

- Costs – up-front charges and commission eat up much of the money in the early years, so cash-in values can be poor
- Inflexibility – if you no longer need your policy, you will be penalised with low surrender values if you wish to pull out before the end of the term
- No tax relief – endowment policies lost their tax relief

in 1984 (although the tax relief at 12.5 per cent remains in place for those taken out earlier)

- Worries – worse than expected investment results coupled with a period of low inflation has meant that some policies will not provide sufficient capital to do their intended job and repay the mortgage at the end of the term. Policy-holders in these circumstances need to make extra financial provision
- Age-sensitive – endowment policies are more expensive the older you are when you take them out

Personal Equity Plans (PEPS)

An increasingly popular backing for interest-only mortgages

is the personal equity plan (PEP). Introduced in 1987, PEPs are a tax-free investment. You can have PEPs linked directly to individual shares or, as most people prefer, have them linked to unit trusts or investment trusts. There is no income tax to be paid on dividends and no capital gains tax to be paid on any profits at the end of the day.

No more than £6,000 in each tax year (running from 6 April to the following 5 April) can be invested in a general PEP, although another £3,000 each tax year can be put into a single company PEP. You can use either type of PEP or both to build up the capital owing on your home loan.

Your monthly PEP payments, designed to pay off the loan over a set number of years, is based on the figure that your PEP manager assumes the stock market will grow by. Currently this will be either 6 or 12 per cent. Different assumptions can make a big difference to how much you pay, as the table below shows:

Mortgage	Length	Monthly contributions based on a growth rate of	
		6 per cent	12 per cent
£		£	£
50,000	20 years	120	61
	25 years	82	34
60,000	20 years	144	72
	25 years	97	41
70,000	20 years	176	84
	25 years	113	47
80,000	20 years	191	96
	25 years	129	53
90,000	20 years	214	107
	25 years	145	59

100,000	20 years	238	118
	25 years	160	66
120,000	20 years	284	142
	25 years	192	78
150,000	20 years	355	177
	25 years	239	97
180,000	20 years	425	211
	25 years	286	116
200,000	20 years	472	235
	25 years	318	128

Source: *Fleming Investment Trust Services*

The advantages of using a PEP to repay your mortgage are:

- Low charges – PEPs have low or, in some cases, non-existent setting up charges, although the initial charge on the underlying unit trust could be between 3–5 per cent so most of the money starts working for you immediately. There is usually an annual management fee of 1–1.5 per cent
- Early cash-in values – these mirror the underlying investments
- Tax-efficient – apart from the fact that you must fund your PEP out of your own taxed income, PEPs are otherwise free of all taxes
- It is easy to increase or, if appropriate, reduce your monthly PEP payment – up to a level of £500 a month
- Early repayment – if investment performance is good, there may be a lump sum, or the loan can be paid off early.

The drawbacks to taking a PEP mortgage are:

- No guarantees – so if the stock market falls, so does the value of the PEP
- Exit charges – to stop PEP-holders cashing in their money there may be modest exit charges for cancelling the PEP within five years
- Limits – only £6,000 a year can be paid into a general PEP, so no extra money can be paid in. However, this ceiling of £500 a month will not affect the majority of borrowers
- No life insurance – borrowers must buy their own life insurance
- Redundancy – there is no state help for borrowers who lose their jobs until the value of their PEPs is less than £8,000

Pension plans

Borrowers are able to earmark part or all of the tax-free cash lump sum they will get from their pension at retirement to pay off the mortgage. As pension plan contributions are tax free (up to a generous level) and the mortgage itself attracted tax relief, pension mortgages were at one time very fashionable. However, with the growing realisation that many people will not have sufficient retirement income for a comfortable old age, anything which has the effect of reducing retirement income has to be questioned.

The advantages of a mortgage backed by a pension plan are:

- Tax relief – money paid into a pension is tax free at the individual's highest rate of income tax. A borrower paying basic rate tax will benefit by an extra 23p for every 77p that he pays. A 40 per cent higher rate taxpayer gains 40p for every 60p he pays towards his pension

- Tax-free lump sum – the lump sum paid out by a pension plan (which can be as much as 25 per cent of the entire personal pension fund built up) is tax free. With other types of pension arrangement the lump entitlement could be higher
- Tax-free fund – investments made by your pension plan roll up free of all taxes and so it should grow faster than it otherwise would
- Life insurance is tax free – life insurance bought as part of a pension plan is cheap, as it is also eligible for tax relief

The drawbacks of a mortgage backed by a pension plan are:

- Inflexible – the earliest money can be taken out of a personal pension is at the age of 50, and sometimes later with company pensions. As a result, the mortgage cannot be paid off until then at the earliest and interest must be paid on the loan
- Job-changing problems – care must be taken every time borrowers change jobs to make sure an adequate pension is in place to deal with the loan. This is particularly true for anyone planning to use the cash commutation option of a company pension scheme
- Reduced pension – taking a lump sum cuts the amount of pension income on offer. Borrowers need to make sure they are paying in enough both to pay off the mortgage and to provide a decent pension

HOW THE MONTHLY COSTS COMPARE

The borrower is a 29-year-old man, a non-smoker who is taking out a £50,000 mortgage over a 25-year term. The mortgage interest rate is 7.25 per cent. In the case of the pension mortgage, his mortgage term has been extended to 35 years.

Repayment	
Mortgage repayment	£338.46
Term insurance	£11.46
TOTAL	£349.92
PEP	
Interest payment	£274.91
PEP (assuming growth rate of 6 per cent)	£68.10
Term insurance	£10.18
TOTAL	£353.19
Endowment	
Interest payment	£274.91
Endowment	£80.64
TOTAL	£355.55
Pension	
Interest payment	£274.91
Pension premium	£74.90
Term assurance	£12.96
TOTAL	£362.77

Source: *Halifax*

MIRAS

The tax relief borrowers get on their mortgage payments is

called MIRAS – Mortgage Interest Relief at Source – and has been whittled away over the last few years. The relief is normally included in your monthly payments, although there may be circumstances where it is given through your tax coding. The tax relief is now just 15 per cent on the first £30,000 of the loan. If there is more than one borrower only one of them can get MIRAS relief on their payments. However, it still makes a difference. A £50,000 loan over 25 years with interest at 7.25 per cent with MIRAS costs £276.41 a month to pay. Without MIRAS, that goes up to £303.75 – a saving of over £27 a month.

EXTRA PAYMENTS

Borrowers can pay in any extra money they have to cut the size of their loans. If you want to do this, check with the lender first when extra payments can be made. Not all lenders have good enough computer systems to allow extra cash to be paid in at any time. Instead, they have set days when they will accept extra payments.

It is vital to put the money in on the right day. Often lenders will take extra money paid in on the wrong date and simply put it on one side without paying any interest on it. Borrowers should save the money in a decent interest-bearing account until the money can be paid in.

If you wish to make a one-off lump payment towards reducing your mortgage, check that your planned repayment is sufficient. Some lenders will insist that lump sum extra payments should be at least £1,000–£5,000. If you repay less, the money will reduce your mortgage debt until the beginning of the lender's next accounting year.

WHAT IF I LOSE MY JOB?

Borrowers losing their jobs can get help from the state, but this is only on the interest, not the capital part of the mortgage. This has been cut in recent years:

- Borrowers with loans taken out after October 1995 must wait nine months for any help on the interest element of any loan worth up to £100,000
- Borrowers with mortgages taken out before then get no payments for eight weeks, half their payments paid for the first 16 weeks, then the full amount is paid
- If you have savings of more than £8,000, other than in your pension or endowment policy, then you will not qualify for any help at all

Regardless of how much state help borrowers are entitled to, the first step is to tell the lender. The sooner they are aware and can reschedule your payments, the better. This could also help stop mortgage arrears building up.

ACCIDENT, SICKNESS AND UNEMPLOYMENT INSURANCE

Since the state no longer provides immediate assistance for anyone facing mortgage difficulties as a result of having been made unemployed, accident, sickness and unemployment insurance can be bought from most lenders. This will cover the cost of the mortgage payments, usually for one year. The bigger the loan, the more the insurance will cost. It is possible to cut down the cost of these plans by only taking out accident and sickness or just unemployment cover, but this is not a good idea. People are just as likely to have an accident as lose their jobs, so they could be left dangerously exposed.

As it is a relatively new form of insurance, there is still a wide variation in the terms between companies. You do not have to take the lender's insurance, so shop around and look at the small print to find out exactly when your plan will and will not pay out. Self-employed and contract workers will often have trouble getting a pay-out.

The cost of insuring monthly payments on a 25 year repayment mortgage for 12 months

Borrowers have to wait one month before payments start
ASU = accident, sickness and unemployment;
U = unemployment only;
AS = accident and sickness only

LOAN	MONTHLY BENEFIT	ASU	U	AS
£	£	£	£	£
50,000	350	19.55	14.17	10.58
60,000	450	25.14	18.22	13.61
70,000	500	27.93	20.24	15.12
80,000	550	30.72	22.27	16.63
90,000	650	36.31	26.32	19.65
100,000	700	39.10	28.34	21.17

Source: *Nationwide Building Society*

Make sure the insurance company offering the plan is a member of the Insurance Ombudsman's Bureau. If there is any dispute over a pay-out, the ombudsman will decide whether or not the company should pay the money.

Home owners with endowments who are made redundant should avoid cashing them in. This will give poor value. Instead, insurance companies will make them 'paid up'. This means the money invested is still growing, but no new money is going in. They can be restarted later on.

APPENDIX: REPAYMENT TABLES

Use these tables to calculate how much your mortgage will cost each month at different interest rates. The monthly cost is based on each £1,000 of home loan, so just multiply the cost in the table by the size of your mortgage in thousands.

The figures do not include the tax relief which is given on the interest payments on the first £30,000 of the loan. This relief is given at 15 per cent. On the first £30,000 of the loan the interest cost will be reduced by 15 per cent – but the balance will be at the level quoted below.

Mortgage repayment table per £1,000:
cost of £1,000 of mortgage

INTEREST RATE	YEARS 15 Yrs £ per month	20 Yrs £ per month	25 Yrs £ per month
2.00%	6.49	5.10	4.27
2.25%	6.61	5.23	4.40
2.50%	6.74	5.35	4.53
2.75%	6.86	5.48	4.66
3.0%	6.99	5.61	4.79
3.25%	7.11	5.74	4.92
3.50%	7.24	5.87	5.06

INTEREST RATE	YEARS 15 Yrs £ per month	20 Yrs £ per month	25 Yrs £ per month
3.75%	7.37	6.00	5.20
4.0%	7.50	6.14	5.34
4.25%	7.63	6.27	5.48
4.50%	7.76	6.41	5.62
4.75%	7.90	6.55	5.77
5.0%	8.03	6.69	5.92
5.25%	8.17	6.83	6.07
5.50%	8.31	6.98	6.22
5.75%	8.45	7.12	6.37
6.00%	8.59	7.27	6.52
6.25%	8.73	7.42	6.68
6.50%	8.87	7.57	6.84
6.75%	9.01	7.72	7.00
7.00%	9.15	7.87	7.16
7.25%	9.30	8.02	7.32
7.50%	9.45	8.18	7.48
7.75%	9.59	8.34	7.65
8.00%	9.74	8.49	7.81
8.25%	9.89	8.65	7.98
8.50%	10.04	8.81	8.15
8.75%	10.19	8.97	8.32
9.00%	10.34	9.13	8.49
9.25%	10.50	9.30	8.66
9.50%	10.65	9.46	8.83
9.75%	10.81	9.63	9.01
10.00%	10.96	9.79	9.19
10.25%	11.12	9.96	9.03
10.50%	11.28	10.13	9.54
10.75%	11.43	10.30	9.72

INTEREST RATE	YEARS 15 Yrs £ per month	20 Yrs £ per month	25 Yrs £ per month
11.00%	11.59	10.47	9.90
11.25%	11.75	10.64	10.08
11.50%	11.92	10.81	10.26
11.75%	12.08	10.99	10.45
12.00%	12.24	11.16	10.63
12.25%	12.40	11.34	10.81
12.50%	12.57	11.51	11.00
12.75%	12.73	11.69	11.19
13.00%	12.90	11.87	11.37
13.25%	13.07	12.05	11.56
13.50%	13.23	12.23	11.75
13.75%	13.40	12.41	11.94
14.00%	13.57	12.59	12.13
14.25%	13.74	12.77	12.32
14.50%	13.91	12.95	12.51
14.75%	14.08	13.13	12.70
15.00%	14.26	13.32	12.90
15.25%	14.43	13.09	12.90
15.50%	14.60	13.69	13.28
15.75%	14.78	13.87	13.48
16.00%	14.95	14.06	13.67
16.25%	15.13	14.25	13.87
16.50%	15.30	14.44	14.06
16.75%	15.48	14.62	14.26
17.00%	15.66	14.81	14.46
17.25%	15.83	15.00	14.65
17.50%	16.01	15.19	14.85
17.75%	16.19	15.38	15.05
18.00%	16.37	15.57	15.25

INTEREST RATE	YEARS 15 Yrs £ per month	20 Yrs £ per month	25 Yrs £ per month
18.25%	16.55	15.76	15.45
18.50%	16.73	15.96	15.65
18.75%	16.91	16.15	15.85
19.00%	17.10	16.34	16.05
19.25%	17.28	16.54	16.25
19.50%	17.46	16.73	16.45
19.75%	17.64	16.92	16.65
20.00%	17.83	17.12	16.85

Source: *Council of Mortgage Lenders*

REMEMBER ...

- There are many different types of mortgage and one will be right for you – you can even mix and match different ways of borrowing and repaying to suit your requirements
- There are advantages and disadvantages with all forms of mortgage. Make a careful comparison of the monthly costs
- MIRAS (Mortage Interest Relief at Source) is given on loans up to £30,000. Extra payments can help reduce your repayments or the size of the capital sum outstanding
- If you lose your job, tell your lender straightaway. They may be able to help by rescheduling payments. Some state assistance may also be available
- You can take out insurance to cover your mortgage repayments if for any reason you can no longer make them

9

INSURING YOUR NEW HOME AND CONTENTS

Once you have exchanged contracts to buy your new property, it is vital that you get it properly insured. Unlike car insurance it is not a legal requirement, although mortgage lenders will insist that you have cover for the structure of the property. There are two types of insurance you must buy for your home – buildings and home contents:

- Buildings insurance will be demanded by your mortgage lender. It not only covers you against problems with the fabric of the house, such as subsidence, fire or a collapsing roof, but protects the lender's interest too, as it retains some stake in the property until you have completely repaid the loan
- Home contents insurance is voluntary. It protects your possessions within the home against damage, fire or theft. Special arrangements are made to cover goods such as cameras and sports equipment which are used outside your house

- Buildings and contents cover can be bought in a combined policy

BUYING BUILDINGS AND CONTENTS INSURANCE

It is sensible to shop around for both these types of cover, as policies vary from insurance company to insurance company, with some offering more extensive cover than others. You have a range of insurance companies and organisations to consult. You may wish to let your lender choose the insurance company for you; you can use the services of an insurance consultant to find the best deal for you; or you can buy your insurance direct from an insurance company, usually by telephone.

Lenders

Building societies traditionally arranged the buildings and home contents cover for borrowers who were allocated an insurer from a panel of insurance companies selected by the building society. Later the choice was increased, permitting borrowers to choose which of the companies on the panel they preferred.

Now borrowers have the freedom to choose whichever insurer they wish, regardless of the lender's preferred choice. The insurance arranged through your lender may not be the cheapest, but lenders maintain that, should you have to make a claim, their muscle will help the claim to get settled quickly and without fuss. Some mortgage

lenders will still insist that buildings and sometimes home contents cover is taken out with them – and make it a condition for a lower mortgage interest rate for one or more years.

In this case you should consider the loan on its own merits. If it is worth taking, then you can accept the insurance terms for the duration of the special mortgage deal. But as buildings and contents insurance is arranged on an annual basis, you can shop around for cover which is either cheaper or better or both to take out as soon as you can without penalty. Some building societies will charge a one-off fee, typically £25, if you arrange your buildings insurance elsewhere. However, many of the insurers who are looking for independent business will rebate this charge if you give them your business.

Direct insurers

Direct insurers are a new type of insurance company. They are sometimes known as telephone insurers because that is the way they conduct their business. Such companies have revolutionised the way in which customers take out buildings and contents cover – and helped to bring down the cost of this type of insurance considerably, particularly for standard families.

However, they do concentrate on good risks, which basically comes down to the kind of area you live in, even to the particular street. You may be dismayed to be turned down by a direct insurer, particularly if you have previously made a claim with another company. Inner city and high crime areas are not popular.

Insurance consultant

An independent insurance consultant or broker will be able to obtain quotations from a range of customers for you. This is a particularly useful service for families who live in an unusual house, or have one which might be considered difficult to insure – for example, a thatched cottage – or have had difficulty in obtaining cover elsewhere, perhaps because of a poor claims record. Your adviser should be able to help you if you have to make a claim on a policy he has arranged.

You should use the services of a recognised insurance broker. He will be regulated by the Insurance Brokers Registration Council which means you are covered by a compensation scheme – should things go wrong.

BUILDINGS INSURANCE

Buildings insurance covers you for the cost of rebuilding your home if it is damaged through, for example, fire or flood. If you own a house then you will have to take out the cover yourself. In most cases, buildings insurance will be included in the service charge for people living in flats or maisonettes. This insurance covers you for the cost of rebuilding your home, including the installation of any fixtures or fittings such as bathroom suites or fitted kitchens. The policy will also usually include outhouses such as garages and sheds, but you should check whether boundary walls, garden ornaments and drives, for example, are included.

Remember, it is the cost of rebuilding a property that you are covering so the sum insured will not be the same as the market price you paid for it – in fact, it may well be considerably higher, especially if non-standard materials have been used. To help, the Association of British Insurers (ABI) has produced a guide to the rebuilding costs of your property in conjunction with the Royal Institution of Chartered Surveyors. This tells you how to work out the rebuilding costs yourself, though it is worth having this professionally checked by a surveyor every so often. The major risks the policy will cover you against are fire, lightning, storm and flood, explosion, earthquake, thieves, riot, aircraft and things falling from aircraft, falling trees, landslip, collapse of aerials and water leaks.

There are also some other valuable inclusions:

- Alternative accommodation, up to a prefixed limit, if your home becomes uninhabitable and while repairs are being carried out
- Liability cover, normally up to £1 million. This will cover you as the owner of the property against damage or injury to other people or their property. Your contents insurance will also provide this cover and your main legal liability will be on the contents rather than the buildings insurance if a claim is made
- Cover for underground pipes and cables (for example gas pipes) is included for accidental damage, but not wear and tear
- Glass in doors, windows and skylights is covered against breakage, which is especially valuable for homes with double glazing or unusual size windows

Policy features

- Excess – insurance companies will normally require you to pay the first part of any claim, known as the

excess, and this amount may vary depending on what type of claim you are making

You can ask the company to increase the excess – known as a voluntary excess – in return for a lower premium, but you cannot ask for the excess to be reduced in return for higher premiums. If you choose a voluntary excess for one year you are not stuck with it for life – you can ask for the amount to return to the insurer's standard level at any time, though you may have to pay an extra premium if this is during the policy's lifetime.

- Index-linking – when you are taking out a policy also think about having it index linked – that is, rising by inflation each year. That way, there should not be a shortfall if you have to make a claim. Some policies automatically include index-linking

If your home is an old or unusual property a specialist insurer may be able to provide cover more competitively than a standard one. If your home has ever suffered subsidence this is also likely to cause problems. Find out whether it has been properly treated and bear in mind that you may have to stay with the previous owner's insurer. Most companies will have a separate excess for subsidence, if it is covered at all, especially in high risk areas. Insurance is designed to cover you against unforeseen damage to your property. It is very unlikely to pay out if damage is caused by neglect of the property on your part.

To reduce the likelihood of a claim being turned down:

- Check the roof, gutters and drain pipes regularly and repair any damage as soon as possible
- Make sure pipes and boilers are properly lagged. This

will not only save on heating bills but also reduce the chance of pipes bursting during cold weather. Make sure the loft is adequately insulated as well

- Find out where the main water pipe enters your home and make sure that the stopcock can be turned off easily in the case of flooding. Also find out where electricity and gas enter the home so they too can be turned off in an emergency
- Check that the building is generally in good repair. Extra insurance can be taken out against rot if, for example, the house is timber framed, and is available from specialist insurers such as Rentokil

HOME CONTENTS INSURANCE

No one can force you to cover your possessions, but unless you have a lot of cash that you can use to buy everything afresh, it is a vital insurance to have. Home contents cover will pay out the cost of replacing your furniture and other possessions if they are stolen or damaged by a wide range of causes, including fire and flood. It can be bought as either a stand-alone policy or combined with your buildings insurance. It is entirely up to you which one you choose and where you buy it, provided your mortgage lender does not insist you buy its own insurance as part of a cheap loan. The first thing to do is to work out how much cover you need. The easiest thing to do is to write down the estimated value of your contents room by room – and don't forget the carpets and curtains in this.

There are then some key questions to ask yourself before you buy:

- Do you need extra cover for valuable items such as jewellery, antiques or paintings? Insurers will ask you to itemise expensive possessions – usually those worth more than £1,000 or £1,500. There are several specialist insurers for people with high value possessions, so it is worth shopping around if you fall into this category
- How do you want to pay for cover – monthly or annually? Not every insurer will give you the option and you may have to pay extra for the monthly facility. This also applies to buildings insurance
- Do you want items covered while they are away from home? Choosing this option covers any possessions up to a set value. But it can be a double-edged sword when it comes to travel insurance, as a claim for lost

luggage while abroad may be split between the home contents and travel insurer – known as subrogation – and you could lose any no claims discount. On the flip side, though, some travel insurers offer a discount if personal possessions are excluded from a policy

- Do you want cover index-linked, which means it automatically increases by the cost of living each year so you are not caught short if you make a claim?
- Most insurers offer a range of discounts off the standard premiums if, for example, you are over a certain age, have an alarm and/or security lights, have a smoke detector fitted, belong to your local Neighbourhood Watch Scheme, or have not made a claim for a year or two. Alarms must be fitted by a National Approved Council for Security Systems (NACOSS)-approved fitter to qualify
- Do you want all risks accidental damage cover? This will cover you against damage caused by accident, such as spilling bleach on a carpet or knocking over an expensive vase
- Window and door locks may be a condition of cover, so make sure that your home has them and that they work properly. An insurer may not pay out in a theft claim if there is no sign of forced entry
- If you do make a claim, what type of service do you want? Some companies have link-ups with suppliers and will replace goods for you rather than you having to shop around, while others will give you the cash and allow you to choose what you replace. Be careful, though – some companies may scale down the cash option by the amount of discount they could get if they replaced the items for you

- Most policies have a 24-hour helpline, giving advice if, for example, a pipe should burst at three in the morning. Is this important? What about a 24-hour legal helpline? Many policies also have some legal expenses cover as standard, which can be used to cover legal costs for any dispute, not just home-related ones
- Make sure the individual levels of cover within the policy are high enough. For example, if freezer cover is included, will the payout cover the value of the food in your freezer should it all be spoilt?

Types of contents insurance

There are four main types of home contents policies:

- New for old – this is the most common form of contents insurance. You tell your insurer the value of your possessions at today's prices, so when you come to claim you are covered for the actual cost of replacement rather than the amount that was originally paid for the item. The only exception is that linen and clothing will have an amount deducted from the value for wear and tear
- Indemnity – this is the cheapest type of cover. You tell your insurer how much your possessions are worth, taking into account any wear and tear. When you claim, you are paid out the value as new, less a little for wear and tear (depending on the item's age), so you basically get the value of the item when it was broken or stolen, regardless of the actual cost of replacing it at current prices. With this type of policy you will almost always be out of pocket if you have to make a claim
- Bedroom-rated – this is an increasingly popular type of

home contents insurance. The insurer sets the level of cover you have based on the number of bedrooms in your home. This type of policy is only a good idea if you do not have unusual or expensive items such as antiques, which could push you above the preset limit

- Unlimited cover – this is the newest form of insurance. The insurer sets the premium rate and there is no maximum sum assured, though there will be limits to the amounts that can be claimed for individual items. It is a good idea for most people as they do not have to work out, and run the risk of underestimating, the value of their contents. But people with low value contents may find themselves paying for extra for insurance they do not need

If you choose to have your contents linked to your buildings cover then the type of cover could be any one of the above, though it is usually new-for-old. The main difference is that the value of the contents is usually set as a percentage of the rebuilding cost of the property rather than based on your estimated value.

Getting the right level of cover is vital, as is keeping your insurer informed if you make any structural changes such as extensions, which increase the value of the property, or buy any valuable new possessions. Insurers are well within their rights to scale down a claim for both buildings and home contents if you are underinsured by the amount of the underinsurance, so you could be left to find the extra money yourself if this is the case.

Also make sure that you read the policy documents carefully, query any parts you do not understand, and get questions confirmed in writing. Remember: finding out what is not covered by a policy is as important as knowing what is.

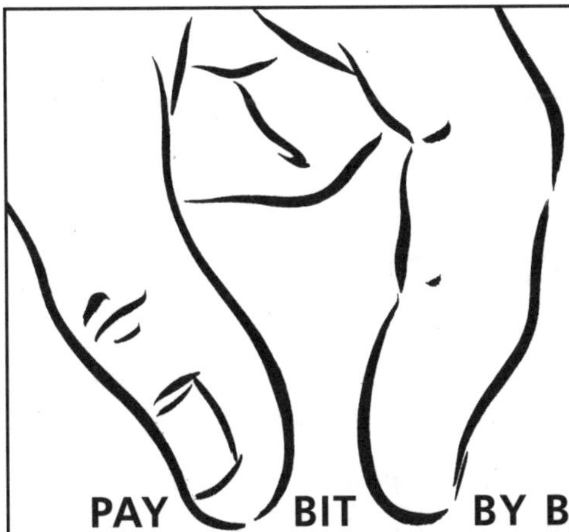

REMEMBER ...

- You will need buildings and contents insurance – shop around, as terms for both vary widely
- Direct insurers offer competitve premiums, but often cannot afford to cover anything other than good risks
- Insurance consultants can help home owners with unusual properties, or those who are having difficulty getting cover
- Check that your buildings insurance is sufficient to cover the cost of rebuilding – it also includes the cost of alternative accommodation and legal liability
- Check the excess on your policy and whether it can be index-linked
- Home contents insurance is not mandatory, but is nevertheless vital. Check you have sufficient cover and that it's the right type – new-for-old, indemnity, bedroom-rated or unlimited
- Neglecting your property could seriously jeopardise your chances of a pay-out
- Knowing what's not covered is as important as knowing what is

10

PAYING THE BILLS

BUYING a house involves far more than just paying the mortgage and insurance bills every month. Exactly where a house is situated will determine the size of a whole host of bills, some of them one-offs, others paid each month. Council tax bills vary in size from area to area and are also dependent on the value of the property. Gas may have to be installed, along with telephone lines. Home owners buying flats on a leasehold basis will also be faced with bills for maintenance costs as well as ground rent.

In many cases you will not have much say in the costs of these basic bills. However, it is possible to appeal against, say, council tax banding and in the future an increasing number of people will be able to choose a gas or electricity supplier to suit their purse. You can already shop around for the cheapest provider of telecom services for particular needs.

COUNCIL TAX

The amount paid in council tax depends largely on the local authority within whose jurisdiction your home is situated.

Within certain limits laid down by central government, it is up to the local council to set the level of tax as they see fit.

As a general rule of thumb the more deprived the area the higher the council tax will be, as the authority has to provide more social services. The amount of council tax paid is also based on the saleable value of the property on 1 April 1991. Depending on their valuation, properties will fall into one of eight council tax bands. Any subsequent rise or fall in the market value of those properties is not taken into account. These valuations were fixed by teams of valuers (often from local estate agencies) reporting to the Inland Revenue. There was no possibility of each house being individually assessed, so anomalies in valuation have occurred. The eight valuation bands for England are:

- up to £40,000 — Band A
- over £40,000 and up to £52,000 — Band B
- over £52,000 and up to £68,000 — Band C
- over £68,000 and up to £88,000 — Band D
- over £88,000 and up to £120,000 — Band E
- over £120,000 and up to £160,000 — Band F
- over £160,000 and up to £320,000 — Band G
- over £320,000 — Band H

When the eight bands were originally worked out there was a spate of appeals against the valuations applied to particular properties. Now such appeals are rare. If one happens it is because something like a motorway has been built near a house, drastically bringing down its value. Major alterations to a home can also affect its value so much that it could be moved up into the next tax banding. If this happens the current owner is not affected. But once it is sold, the new owner may well find that their new home moves up into the next band.

People aged over 18 are liable to pay council tax. There is no distinction made between tenants, freeholders and leaseholders – all must pay it. If a property has joint owners the bill will only go to one of them, but both owners are responsible for paying the tax. To find out who should pay, local authorities send out forms to residents which must be filled in and returned. There is a £50 penalty for not returning the form.

- Single home owners can get a 25 per cent discount. For this to happen the owner must apply to the local authority
- If a property is not a principle residence and is left unoccupied, then the tax is halved
- The council tax bill does not rise if there are more than two adults living in a home
- The local authority will pursue residents for any late payments, often through the local magistrates' court

Discounts are also on offer for the disabled. If they are eligible, this will have the effect of putting the property into a lower and therefore less expensive valuation band. This happens if:

- It can be shown that an extra room (other than a kitchen or bathroom) is necessary for the disabled person
- An extra kitchen or bathroom is needed or

- Extra space is needed in the home for wheelchair access

Appeals

If for any reason a home owner thinks a council tax bill is wrong, there is an appeals process to sort it out. This is separate from any appeal against the valuation which deals with the property's banding. There are three grounds for an appeal:

- The council is sending the bill to the wrong person for that home
- The property should be exempt from council tax
- No discount has been given, so the bill is wrong

The first step is to write to the local authority giving the reasons for the appeal. In this first stage, the authority then has two months to deal with the appeal. If you are still unhappy with the decision given or have received no reply in the two months, you can go to a valuation tribunal. Disgruntled taxpayers have two months to go to the tribunal from the date they receive the disputed decision, or four months from the date of the original complaint if they have had no reply.

The complainant must outline in writing the the decision being appealed against, along with the reasons for rejecting that decision. If all sides agree, the case can be sorted out by an exchange of written representations to the the tribunal. If not, there is a formal hearing. Before any hearing the valuation tribunal will send out a leaflet explaining the procedure. The hearing will not last more than a day and is free to use. The only cost comes if you, the complainant, decide to employ a solicitor. If the appeal is successful the council tax bill will be amended. It is important to keep on paying the original bill during the appeals process, otherwise there could be a penalty for late payment.

TELEPHONE

Most homes have an existing telephone line. If this is the case but the previous owners have had it disconnected, British Telecom (BT) will charge £9.99 for reconnection. If the sellers are still there while the mortgage deal is going through, it should be possible to put the existing number into the new name free of charge. The new owner just rings BT and tells them the date to switch over names.

If there is no telephone line at all in a property, which can happen if a barn is converted or a derelict property renovated, then there is a charge of up to £99.99 to have a line put in by BT. £99.99 is the absolute ceiling for the cost. BT will not give a timescale for putting in a line, as that will depend on where the property is. Most new homes have lines put in by the builders, so there should only be the £9.99 reconnection charge to pay.

Before you decide on using BT for your telephone service, shop around. For the last 12 years the telecoms market has been open to competition and there are many other providers such as Mercury, Energis, Ionica and the cable network companies all vying for your business.

Discounts are the order of the day and, depending on when and how much you use your telephone, there are ways and means of cutting down your bills. Other companies may also offer cheaper line rental than BT. Often the new providers aim to undercut BT's discounts by a set percentage. Other services, such as BT's Friends and Family scheme, also let you save money on your most frequently used numbers. For details ring BT on 150.

OTHER BILLS

For all utility bills (such as gas, electricity and water) home owners must make sure they get accurate readings of all the meters the day they move into their new homes. They must also tell their respective utility companies they have taken over the bills and what the meter readings are. This will stop disputes arising later on.

To smooth out the monthly bills suppliers such as British Gas Trading and British Telecom set up special budget accounts. At the start of each year you agree with your supplier your monthly payments and you pay a set amount into the account each month by direct debit.

The monthly payment should then cover the cost of your regular bills. In winter months, for example, heating bills may be higher than the monthly amount paid in. But come summer, the amount left over from lower bills should cover the deficit. At the end of each year the company checks to see if the monthly payments are sufficient. If not, with your agreement, they will increase the monthly payments. British Gas recommends that a budget account should be set up if your bills come to over £80 a year. For amounts lower than that, other ways of paying may be more cost-effective.

Gas

Not every home is connected to gas. Putting in a gas supply from scratch can mean some hefty bills. Where a home has an existing gas pipeline, but for some reason it has been disconnected, it ought to be a fairly cheap and simple job to reconnect it.

Where there is no pipeline, the cost can spiral into thousands of pounds and take several weeks. The cost will depend on how far the property is from an existing gas supply. If it is in a town or city, this should not be too much of a problem. But connection can take time if roadworks are involved in putting down a pipe. If the property is in a remote rural area and the gas supply is some miles away, a lengthy and therefore costly pipline may have to be laid to bring in the supply.

As well as checking out the gas supply to the house, new home owners can get a full safety check of pipes and appliances in the home carried out by British Gas. The Celsia Gas Safety Inspection will be carried out by one of its qualified engineers. All internal pipes, as well as any gas appliances, will be thoroughly checked both for safety and heat efficiency. It costs £59.99 plus VAT. To set one up, ring British Gas Home Energy on the telephone number at the top of the gas bill. Any changes carried out as a result of a visit should be done by a Corgi-registered engineer. And remember, always get a written quote before the work starts.

This whole process will get a bit more complicated in 1998 as the entire gas market is to be opened up to competition and customers will have a choice of gas suppliers. This process began in the West Country in 1996 and should bring down bills, although it might make the situation a bit more confusing.

Electricity

Just about all properties are now connected up to the electricity supply, so home owners are unlikely to encounter the kind of difficulties that can beset gas customers.

The regional electricity companies are responsible for getting the power to the house, but not for the internal wiring. That is down to the home owner or, for communal areas in blocks of flats, the building's freeholder.

Customers concerned that bills are too high can get their local company to run a check. But a word of warning: electricity companies are always unwilling to admit there could be anything wrong with the electricity meter, and may blame a power-hungry appliance instead. Some electricity companies do sell appliances and if that is the case, will probably send out engineers to check that they are in good working order. If this is not the case, get in touch with a qualified electrician.

As a rule, beware of second-hand appliances that come with a house. Check that washing machines, fridges and freezers have the kite mark sign and conform to British Standard BS3456.

Like the gas industry, the electricity market is to be opened up to national competition in 1998. Customers will be able to choose the company that supplies them and hopefully bills will fall.

FLATS

Flats are usually bought on a leasehold basis. This means that their owners will have to pay the freeholder who owns the entire building service charges for looking after the fabric of the building as well as servicing the communal areas. This can include tending the garden as well as the usual ground rent and service charges. The search carried out by the solicitor will show what these bills are. Solicitors should check the level of bills over the last few years to see if they have fluctuated at all and whether they seem reasonable. The level of these charges should be looked at in conjunction with the valuer's report. This will contain comments on how well the freeholder, or managing agent, does the job. Flat owners can then decide whether the bills are fair. If at a later date the freeholder makes a big increase in any of the bills which doesn't seem to be justified by the work being carried out, leaseholders can take them to a free leasehold valuation tribunal to rule on whether or not it is a fair charge.

BUDGET ACCOUNTS

Another way of dealing with all the bills that come in is to set up a special budget account with a bank or building society to pay them. These work in a similar way to suppliers' budget accounts. To do this, work out the cost of all the bills over the year. Then pay in that amount each month. Variable direct debits and standing orders can then take care of the monthly and quarterly bills. If there is a particularly heavy set of bills in any one month, that should be smoothed out by lower bills in following months. It is a good idea to budget for slightly more than the total amount to take care of unexpected extras, such as higher heating bills in very cold weather.

REMEMBER ...

- If you are a single householder, you may be able to claim a council tax discount. If the bill is wrong, or you think your property is in the wrong band, you can appeal
- Shop around for your telephone – there are many different providers vying for trade, and they will offer some very competitive deals
- Take accurate meter readings the day you move into your new property, and let the utility companies know
- British Gas can carry out a full check on your gas supply and any appliances, for safety and fuel efficiency, which could save you money in the long run
- Electricity companies can also run checks if your bills seem to be too high
- Your solicitor's search and the valuer's report will tell you whether the service charges on your flat are fair. If not, you can appeal to the leasehold valuation tribunal
- Setting up a budget account to pay your bills by direct debit or standing order could make life much simpler

11

MAKING ALTERATIONS AND IMPROVEMENTS

Everyone has their own ideas on what makes a perfect property. Even if you buy a house in pristine condition, there will generally be some changes you want to make. These usually fall into two broad categories – immediate minor repairs and decoration and major permanent structural changes.

IMMEDIATE ALTERATIONS

- It is much easier to renovate a house if it is empty. Consider delaying the completion on your existing property for a short period to enable work to be carried out – you will need a short-term bridging loan
- If the property you are buying is empty, see if the present owners will allow work to start as soon as contracts are exchanged
- The mortgage lender may insist on certain work being done immediately. For example, a new damp-proof

course might be made a condition of the loan and some of the mortgage cash will be held back until you have had the work done

- Before you start, work out a schedule so that the jobs can be tackled in the right order. For example, new wiring and plumbing should be installed before decorating takes place
- Locate important aspects such as the stop cock, central heating controls and fuse box before you start work

MAJOR WORKS

There are a variety of questions you should ask before you start on a major home improvement project :

- Can I afford it? You may have to take out an additional mortgage or personal loan so work out your budget carefully. Home improvement loans are available from both banks and building societies. It often makes sense to borrow the extra money from your mortgage provider as it will usually mean lower fees. Typically the value of your home improvement loan plus your mortgage should not exceed 90 per cent of the value of your property and you can usually repay the loan either over a minimum five-year period or a longer period, with the cut-off date coinciding with your final mortgage repayment date. Charges vary but, typically, the cost of a home improvement loan is in line with mortgage rates. Most lenders insist you take out life insurance cover so look through the fine print and make sure you know about any 'extras' before you sign

on the dotted line. There is often an administration fee and it can be worth negotiating hard with your mortgage provider to see if they will reduce upfront charges. You might have to have the home revalued and incur extra valuation and legal fees – it depends on how recently you bought the property and the mortgage provider's rules

- Is it necessary? Some works are vital – for example, a new roof or a damp-proof course. Other alterations may be undertaken to improve the cosmetic appearance of a property or the overall quality of life
- Will it add to the value of the property? Many alterations add little or no value in the short term. You have to stay in the property for a number of years before you reap any rewards. However, there are exceptions to this rule.

There are other points to bear in mind:

- Fashions change. What may be a trendy kitchen today could be out of date in a few years time.
- Do not over-improve your house. Most areas have a prevailing price range and extra improvements may be very poor value. For example, extending a three-bedroom house to four bedrooms may make it stick out like a sore thumb, especially if all the other houses have three bedrooms
- Keep the alterations in character with the locality. For example, you may be allowed to stone-clad the front, but will it fit in?
- Balance the cost and the hassle factor of major alterations against the cost of moving to another house which has everything you want

HOME IMPROVEMENTS

The most popular home improvement is double glazing, followed by a new kitchen, an extra bathroom or toilet, a porch extension, a conservatory, an extra bedroom, a loft conversion, a lounge extension and, finally, stone cladding.

Not all these improvements will actually add value to your home. According to a recent survey of property valuers carried out by the National Westminster Bank, the improvement most likely to add to the resale value of a home is an extra bedroom, followed by an extra bathroom. New kitchens are, according to valuers, likely to cost more than they actually add in value to the house, as are loft conversions, lounge extensions, double glazing and a porch extension. And if you are thinking of stone-cladding, forget it –

Complete NEXUS kitchen in birch veneer finish
£1696
Price valid until 10th August 1997
(Excludes appliances & accessories)

It's Not So Much The Smell Of Baking Bread. It's What It's Baking In.

Not that we're suggesting that those little tricks of the trade don't work. Or that double glazing, central heating and how close the shops are aren't important. It's just that when you've seen the Nexus kitchen, with its stylish design, beech veneer cabinets and acres of storage space, they don't seem quite so important.

But if the house you've set your heart on doesn't feature a Nexus, don't worry. At just **£1696**, you won't need a second mortgage to afford one.

Which also means that if you're selling rather than buying, the Nexus is a realistic alternative to a lick of paint or the ubiquitous hot loaf. Not to mention more effective.

You can take your kitchen home today, or for a small extra charge we can arrange to have it delivered to your home.

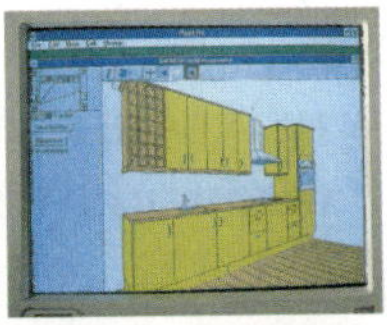

With our free 3D planning system you can see exactly how your new kitchen will look in your home.

Install your kitchen yourself using the easy-to-follow instructions or for an extra charge let our expert installers do it for you.

IKEA®

The home furnishings store from Sweden.

IKEA LEEDS Tel: Kitchen Dept. 01924 427 668 **IKEA BRENT PARK WEMBLEY** Tel: Kitchen Dept. 0181 233 2224 **IKEA CROYDON** Tel: Kitchen Dept. 0181 710 0019 **IKEA WARRINGTON** Tel: Kitchen Dept. 01925 642 270 **IKEA GATESHEAD** Tel: Kitchen Dept. 0191 461 1135 **IKEA BIRMINGHAM** Tel: Kitchen Dept. 0121 568 6735 **IKEA THURROCK** Tel: Kitchen Dept. 01375 302 150 virtually all valuers asked in the survey said that it adds less value than the actual cost.

Garden improvements are becoming more and more popular, according to the Halifax Building Society, with a growing number of customers taking out loans to pay for work to enhance the gardens. If you are looking for a landscape gardener the best way is by personal recommendation. Go and see some of the other gardens he or she has designed and ask the home owner whether the work was done quickly and efficiently and to the agreed timescale. You should ask for a plan showing how they envisage landscaping your garden, although you might find some will insist on a fee, refundable if you go ahead with the work. Too many landscape gardeners have come up with plans only to find home owners do the work themselves, having had a 'design' drawn up for them completely free. Most landscape gardeners ask for a percentage of the agreed price up front – they often have to buy bricks, tiles, plants, etc, as soon as they start on your job, so it is quite reasonable that they are given an 'advance'. However, make sure you do not pay the full price until the work is completed to your complete satisfaction, otherwise you have no comeback if you are unhappy about the way the job has been done. Make sure too that you get everything in writing, spelling out when payments are to be made and what quantity and type of materials are to be used. This estimate should also make it quite clear what is and what is not included in the price.

If you are thinking of having a swimming pool installed, be warned that valuers often say they can even detract from the value of the house. Many people see them as a nuisance requiring a high level of maintenance for little reward, especially during a typical British summer.

PLANNING PERMISSION AND BUILDING REGULATIONS

There are two important aspects to consider before undertaking structural alterations and improvements – planning permission and building regulations.

Planning permission

Many structural alterations need planning approval. The most common include:

- Flat or maisonette extensions
- Dividing part of your house for use as a separate home
- Converting part of your house for business or commercial purposes
- Extending your house. The rules here are quite complicated. Basically, you will need planning approval if the volume is increased by 15 per cent or 70 cubic metres. In addition, permission will be required if the extension is higher than original roof or puts the overall property nearer to a road. There are different and more restrictive rules for listed buildings and properties in conservation areas. You do not usually need to get planning permission for internal alterations, such as replacing windows, painting and decorating the house, putting in roof lights or re-roofing. A loft extension may not require permission if it does not increase the overall volume, but it will if you want to alter a roof which faces a highway. Planning applications are controlled by the local council. The objective is to make sure that any changes fit in with existing surroundings

Diamond

Clean up with Flotex

FLOTEX flooring is renow for its practicality and durability – but now it's a making a fashion statemen

Waterproof, easy to clean and extremely hard wearing - Flotex is the perfect floorcovering for kitchens, bathrooms, conservatories, children's playrooms and hallways.

But now it's also making a fashion statement!

Four new designs have been launched into the established *Home Solutions* collection, bringing dynamic colours and vibrant hues to bear on the most contemporary Flotex designs to date.

Mazara

Geneva

Geneva, inspired by the current trend for introducing brighter colours into the home, has tonal shades which have been highlighted with flecks of contrasting colour - for an ultra-modern design. It's available in four exciting colourways: Emerald, Opal, Amber and Sapphire.

Raffia, influenced by the natural and classic floorcovering material Sisal, is available in a rustic Barley colourway. With a simple knot weave design, it provides an overall eye-catching effect.

Diamond, meanwhile, takes its cue from Coir - another highly popular natural material - but a striking diamond weave design and Oatmeal colourway adds both warmth and texture to the design.

Mazara combines an in vogue mosaic effect and a traditional key square, for an exquisite design that has class written all over it.

The strong, earthy tones of terracotta combined with blue and rich red, or lush green with stone and beige, allow for a more flexible approach to interior design and colour co-ordination.

Clean Scene

The real beauty of Flotex, however, is that by following a few very simple cleaning procedures, it can be returned to its initial condition time after time.

What's more, it's also guaranteed for an impressive 10 years wear!

For day to day care, Flotex just r vacuuming regularly as you wou with any other carpet. Set the br to "low" to brush any dirt and flu out of the pile.

Everyday and stubborn stains po problem either. Paint, crayon, bl ink, cooking fat, coffee, red wine tomato sauce, oil (to name but a can all be removed quickly and e using the "scrape, scrub and rins technique that is unique to Flote

Scrape up a stain or spill straigh away. Use a spatula or blunt edg scraper. And don't be frightened really scraping hard; it won't har your Flotex one bit.

Scrub the stained area with a ha bristled brush using a very weak water/detergent solution - one teaspoon of detergent to five litre water (nearly nine pints).

Rinse thoroughly with clean wa remove all the detergent. This is important. Scrape as much exces water as you can into a cloth. Th just leave your Flotex to dry naturally.

If you'd like to know more abou Flotex flooring - and the new ra - then ask for a free brochure e by writing to: Bonar & Flotex, Freepost (DY114), High Holbor Road, Ripley, Derbyshire, DE5 or by telephoning 01773 74412

FLOTEX

A Bonar product

and do not affect your neighbours. Before putting in an application, discuss your plans with the neighbours. In any case, the council will notify them or put a notice up outside your property

- Discuss your needs with the planning office. They can advise you on the forms required and the fees involved
- If there are problems, you can submit an outline application first before submitting detailed drawings
- Government guidelines suggest that the council should decide the application within eight weeks
- If you are unsure whether permission is required, do not start work until you have consulted the planning authority. They have the power to force you to return a property to its original state
- If permission is refused, the council has to give detailed reasons. Changing your plans may make a difference. If you think the council has acted unreasonably, you can appeal to the Secretary of State at the Department of the Environment

The Department of the Environment produces a useful booklet, Planning – a Guide for Householders, which is available free from local councils.

Building Regulations

New building work may have to conform with building regulations. They lay down minimum standards for items such as building materials, health and safety and fire precautions as well as sewers and drainage. They apply to new buildings, extensions and alterations. Copies are available at local planning offices, although a layman will certainly need the help of an architect or surveyor to interpret them.

Some building work does not need approval. This includes repairs, replacing drains, new bathrooms and fitting central heating, where no major structural alterations are needed. The local authority will be able to tell you if approval is required and how to apply.

Covenants

These are restrictions placed on the property, probably when the house was first built. For example, you may not be able to use the premises for business purposes or park a caravan in the drive. They may limit future development or alterations. Some covenants are unreasonable and therefore unenforceable, but you will need to consult a solicitor to make sure. Mortgage documents may have a restrictive clause stipulating that the lender must be consulted before substantial alterations take place.

GRANTS

The grants system has recently been redesigned and there are a variety of grants available to assist with property improvements.

Renovation Grants

These are available from the local council to both owner-occupiers and landlords. Properties under 10 years old are not eligible and second or holiday homes do not usually

qualify. For owner-occupiers the grant is calculated by way of a means test which assesses how much, if anything, the owner should contribute. The test is based on average weekly income, taking into account savings above £5,000.

Grants to landlords are at the discretion of the council. Landlords generally have to agree to let the property for five years after the grant or repay the money. Applications should be sent to the housing or environmental health department of the local council.

Common Parts Grant

These are discretionary grants from the local council to help repair the common parts of a building containing one or more flats, such as a mansion block or a converted house.

HMO Grant

Only landlords can apply for this grant, which covers a house in multiple occupation where the occupants do not form part of a single household.

Disabled Facilities Grant

This grant is available to let disabled people live more independently in their home. Although it is means tested, the grant can be mandatory for essential adaptations.

Home Repair Assistance

A discretionary grant designed to provide practical help

either in cash or by supplying materials. It is intended for small-scale works with help limited to £2,000 per application or £4,000 over a three-year period.

Explanatory leaflets are available from the Department of the Environment Publications Despatch Centre, tel: 0181 691 9191.

THE PROFESSIONALS

If you are doing a reasonable amount of work, or there are complications, it will certainly be advisable to employ an expert such as an architect or a building surveyor. They both offer a wide range of services, including planning applications, preparing designs and arranging contracts with a builder.

Architects

Although there is no obligation to join, most architects belong to the Royal Institute of British Architects (RIBA). All architects have to be registered with the Architects Registration Council of the UK. Personal recommendation is generally the best way of finding one although your local council may keep a list of local architects. In addition, RIBA will be able to let you have a list of members in your locality as well as leaflets describing the services on offer.

- Fees – these will be decided by the complexity of the work. There could be a flat fee plus local council costs, or an hourly rate. Larger projects are often charged as a percentage of the total cost. Always agree fees at the outset and get a written contract or quotation. If any extra work needs to be done, always get a quote before agreeing that this can go ahead

- If the work is extensive or complicated, make sure the architect carries professional indemnity insurance. If there are problems, it will be difficult to bring a claim against an uninsured person
- If you are applying for a council grant, fees can be included in the total cost

Building surveyors

The Royal Institution of Chartered Surveyors (RICS) can supply a list of local members. In addition, it provides an advisory service on what is needed for a particular job, as well as a possible scale of fees. If you had a structural survey when you bought the property, the surveyor should be able to advise on building work.

Design Consultants

They may not be professionally qualified, but carry out work similar to architects. They often specialise in supervising building projects from start to finish. You should ask if they have professional indemnity insurance.

FINDING A BUILDER

The best way to find a builder is by personal recommendation. You may then be able to inspect the finished product

MARCH INTO SPRING WITH SC JOHNSON WAX

. Spring just around the corner it's
itely time to knuckle down to the
ded Spring cleaning! But how do you
n to get rid of months of dust and grime
get your house back into shape looking
l **and** smelling fresh? Luckily help is at
l thanks to SC Johnson Wax the leading
ehold cleaning products manufacturer
h has produced a list of top tips to take
train out of your cleaning.

ning the whole house can often be a
ting prospect so why not call
ohnson Wax to the rescue and let old
urites like Mr Muscle, Pledge, Glade
Toilet Duck do all the work.

Down . . . Banish all those dusty
ces with new anti-static Pledge Clean
Dust and you'll soon have all your
iture looking clean and shiny.

eath Of Fresh Air . . . After the long winter months treat yourself to the fine fragrances of
de Floriental aerosols and transport your home to the exotic east.

Mr Muscle Take The Strain This Spring . . . Mr Muscle Kitchen Cleaner is now available with a
lemon freshness. Effectively cutting through grease and grime it comes in a handy trigger
y for a speedy application and simply loves the jobs you hate! Also in the Muscle range try
extra power *Sink and Plughole Unblocker* guaranteed to open the toughest of blockages
ng germs and deodourising along the way.

e Your Toilet Bleach Power . . . Get tough on your toilet this Spring with new toilet duck
ch power blocks. Each block comes with 20% active bleach ingredients to provide bleach with
y flush leaving your toilet a clean and germ free zone.

e Power To The Consumer Elbow . . . Duck offers additional benefits to your toilet with 100%
scale Destroyer. More effective than any other product on the market it powers through
scale leaving behind sparkling toilets with a delightful fresh fragrance.

e Your Home An Essence Of Nature This Spring . . . Leave the cold winter evenings behind
enjoy the fresh scent of magnolia and vanilla in your home this spring with Glade candles.
available in Spring Pourri and Peach.

**For further information please contact: Caroline Wray/Tilly McMaster,
Edelman PR Worldwide. Tel: 0171 344 1200. Fax: 0171 344 1222**

and form your own opinion. However, if you are new to the area, neighbours or estate agents may be able to help.

- Get two or three quotes from reputable firms. If you are applying for a grant, the local council will certainly insist on this

- It may pay to choose firms which belong to a trade organisation. For example, the Building Employers Confederation and the Federation of Master Builders both run guarantee schemes insuring against faulty workmanship

- Keep a notebook or other written record of all the decisions you make and the names, addresses and 'phone numbers of suppliers and tradespeople

- Remember that some items have a long delivery period, so you may need to order them well in advance, perhaps as soon as contracts are exchanged

- Make sure you get a written quotation, spelling out exactly what work is to be done. If along the way you decide to have extra work done, don't just ask the builder to do it: make sure that you got a written quotation for the extra work and agree the price, otherwise you could find you get a massive 'extras' bill when the job is completed

- The builder will normally ask for stage payments as the job goes along. This should be spelt out in the written quotation, specifying what percentage of the total contract price has to be paid and at which particular stage. Make sure that you do not pay the bill in full

until the work is completely finished and you are happy with it. If you pay before completion you leave yourself open to problems

In a recent survey by the Halifax Building Society, three-quarters of customers who had recently had building work done said that the work was undertaken and completed on time. One in four said the work took longer than expected, while almost a fifth said they would probably not want to have building work done again. However, virtually all customers claimed the disruption was worth it when it was actually finished.

CONTROLLING THE COWBOYS

Britons spend more than £8.5 billion a year on DIY, home improvements, decorating and general maintenance. There are large numbers of cowboy builders and rogue traders who get up to some very devious tactics to make sure they get a slice of this enormous cake. Some of their methods are not only illegal but dangerous and can place some sections of the community, such as the elderly, at considerable risk. Some of the tricks include:

- Offering to do unnecessary work, especially for the elderly
- Giving artificially low estimates, which have no legal standing, and then inflating the bills
- Offering discounts in exchange for up-front payments, then disappearing
- Giving guarantees which are totally worthless

COMPLAINTS

If you have a complaint, you can approach the local trading standards officer at your council. However, there are a variety of steps you can take to avoid the cowboys:

- Use a local firm which comes well recommended by friends or neighbours
- Get several estimates – although in an emergency this may not always be possible
- Use the helpline recommendations from your contents policy insurer
- Never use a firm which knocks on your door out of the blue, especially after heavy storms or rain
- Get a detailed written estimate
- Check if the firm belongs to a trade organisation. If in any doubt, check with the organisation that the firm is still a member
- Is there a guarantee with the work? This will be worthless if the firm goes out of business in the future, unless there is a back-up guarantee from an insurance company
- Remember that the cheapest quote is not necessarily the best

INTERIOR DESIGN

You may be lucky enough to move into a new house which already suits your requirements and doesn't need major structural alterations. There is still plenty of scope for you to

stamp your personality on your new home, though. Here are a few suggestions:

Bathrooms

As the smallest room in the house, bathrooms tend to be the easiest projects to begin with when moving. Fresh paint, appliances, shower curtains, tiles and other bathroom decor offer a reassuringly clean feel when moving into a previously occupied property. Don't be afraid to discard the old avocado green fixtures in favour of new, bright colours or traditional Victorian and Edwardian shades. A power/steam shower can transform an old bathroom, but don't get carried away with an approach that is too minimalist. Installing a shower and eliminating the bath can devalue a property. It might help to consult a specialist who can suggest ways to maximise the space in a small bathroom. The British Bathroom Council is a trustworthy resource; their number is 01782 747074.

Kitchens

The kitchen is likely to become the centre of life at home, so it's important to have a comfortable, convenient space. When looking at a prospective property, try to envision the different new appliances, clean tiles or specialised paint effects can make in the kitchen. Think twice before covering counter tops in tiles – it's impossible to clean spilt sugar from the grout! In a smaller space, consider installing racks overhead for hanging pots and pans. Above all, don't rule out an attractive property just because the refrigerator is too small. There are plenty of ways to create your own culinary

workspace and many companies will customise a kitchen to reflect your lifestyle.

Bedrooms

The bedroom will be your haven and private space. Take some time to consider what you want surrounding you to make you feel relaxed and comfortable. Lighting is very important for dressing areas and reading in bed. Curtains will have a strong effect in your bedroom, and remember that the colours of the paint, upholstery and linens you choose will be the first things you see every morning. When looking at a property do not forget the bulk of bedroom furniture, including beds and wardrobes. You must be confident that you will be able to fit your belongings into the bedroom of a house or flat in such a way that you will not feel crowded or unsettled. Built-in furniture offers an attractive alternative to a 'cluttered' look. There are many experts in the field who can advise you with a free consultation.

Conservatories

A conservatory is one of the easiest and most attractive ways to increase the square footage of a house. It is also an effective way to incorporate natural light into an interior. A survey of home owners has demonstrated that the conservatory ranks as the third most used room in those houses that have them. Depending on the orientation of a conservatory, the natural light you receive will vary. South-facing rooms get sun all year but will require ventilation, while north-facing rooms will require insulation in winter. It will

Your Place
Your Place Furniture UK Ltd.
Cherry Wood and Oak Furniture for Bedroom, Lounge, Dining Room and Study
Sunday & Evening Appointments Welcome
171 High Street, Tooting, London, SW17 Tel/Fax: 0181 767 7496
10 Fauconberg Road, Chiswick, London, W4 Tel/Fax: 0181 747 3030

be useful to consult your local Conservatory Council member on 0171 403 7177 for information about building codes and regulations as well as about the best companies.

Floors

Attractive, sensible floors can turn a house or flat into a stunning space. Floors in kitchens and bathrooms will get wet, so plan accordingly with practical floor coverings like tiles and lino. Wooden floors are becoming extremely popular and new lines are being produced to meet the demand. Remember to protect new floors with padding under furniture to prevent scratching, and consult a supplier about options for protective coatings. The wide selections of carpets increases every year, particularly in terms of the range of quality available. Sisal, hessian and other woven coverings are particularly popular, but it is hard to beat a deep pile carpet for comfort and warmth in a bedroom. Be sure to consider such elements of your lifestyle as children and pets before choosing white carpets or other delicate design elements.

Cleaning

Moving house can be a challenge before you even consider inheriting a previous owner's mess. Make the exercise simpler by having the proper cleaning supplies in hand as you move, both out of your old place and into you new one. You'll be much happier putting dishes and plates away in clean cupboards and arranging furniture in rooms that are tidy and fresh. Moving day may be your only opportunity to clean floors without the obstacles of furniture.

750D Built-in enclosure

800 W Corner enclosure

High street shopping for home furnishings

The high street shops are developing capsule ranges of products in popular colours to help busy home owners create themes that reflect their lifestyles. Whether you prefer colour schemes in bright, modern hues or natural beiges and creams, the expanding selection of household accessories available from the home stores offers affordable style and an opportunity to use your own creativity.

Paint effects

One way to personalise your decor is to choose from a wide range of paint effects. Clouding, marbling, and other texturing techniques can add a unique flair to your interior designs. There are many books on the subject, and representatives at home supply stores can be very helpful.

REMEMBER ...

- It's easier to renovate an empty house – but this means you will need a bridging loan, which could be expensive
- Major works could mean taking out another loan on top of your mortgage, so think carefully about whether the changes are essential or not
- You may need planning permission, or have to ensure that your alterations conform to building regulations – the planning authority can force you to restore the property to its original state if you haven't followed the rules
- Not all 'improvements' add to the value of the house – beware stone-cladding!
- Don't neglect the garden – the best way to find a good landscape gardener is through word of mouth
- You may be able to apply for a grant to assist with the cost of the work
- Fashions change. Keep this in mind as well as the character of the properties which surround yours – making it stick out like a sore thumb could make it much more difficult to sell in the future

12

SELLING YOUR HOME

IF you thought buying your home was stressful, wait until you come to sell it. The problem is made much worse if you are buying and selling at the same time – this can be unbelievably demanding. Most people who are not first-time buyers still end up in this position, despite the growing numbers who choose to sell first and rent for a while before buying under less pressure.

The core of the problem is that the house-buying and selling process is largely outside your control. When several people are buying and selling their homes, all aiming to move on the same day, a chain forms and progress is only made at the pace of the slowest in the chain. The longer the chain, the more likely it is to break down, with sales consequently falling through.

So you've been warned. Even so, there's a lot you can do to keep the selling process from driving you over the edge.

The first major decision you have to make is: should I find a buyer for my home first and then put in an offer on a new home, or do it the other way around? The best answer is, without any doubt at all, to sell your home first – or at least find a firm buyer for it. The major reason is that you are bound to get emotionally involved in the dream home you want to buy but, until you have a buyer for your property, you've no real hope of getting it unless you want to take out an expensive bridging loan. Conversely, if you put in an offer on a property with a buyer already lined up for your home, then you're in a strong position to bargain.

The second decision is whether to sell it yourself, or through an estate agent? The estate agent is the agent for the seller, so this time, he's working for you. But since estate agents charge commission from 1.5 to 3 per cent of the selling price, many people try to do it themselves first. It's perfectly practical to do this – thousands do so each year, saving themselves a lot of money in the process.

SELLING YOUR HOME YOURSELF

- Press advertising – unless your house is in Greater London, a prestigious area, or is in some way special, go for the local rather than the national press. Not only is it much cheaper, but your buyer is statistically more likely to come from the locality rather than the other end of the country. Look at other advertisements in the property section, and arrange for yours to be in a similar style – a photograph helps. The classified advertising department of the paper will usually be willing to help you with this. Put your advertisement in for several weeks
- Word of mouth, and a notice on your workplace noticeboard – this sometimes works, and costs you nothing

- A 'For Sale' board outside your home – people visiting other homes in your area which they have seen through estate agents will see your board. You need to have a phone number on it, and ideally an answering machine at home in case people ring when you're not at home. You can get professionally produced ready-made boards or, if you are handy at carpentry, you can make your own. They must conform with rules governing the size of 'For Sale' boards
- You will need to prepare your own particulars to give to visitors – these will give potential buyers the basic details of the property. Model them on the ones estate agents use and try to follow the same style. Get a decent photograph taken, prepare the words on a word processor, and get your local instant print shop to produce

copies. This is not expensive, and it is worth doing the job properly. Include information on the number of rooms, their sizes, facilities, any main items which will remain, the number of years remaining on the lease if applicable and your council tax band, just as an estate agent would. Remember that, like an agent, you are bound by the law banning misleading descriptions – but it is worth putting a line at the bottom stating that the particulars do not form part of a legally binding contract

- Deciding what will remain when you move is an important issue – in general, it is pointless and uneconomic to remove items such as fitted kitchen and carpets which were designed to fit the house. They probably won't fit the new one. So let them stay and try to factor this into the price

Doing it yourself has the drawback that that you will have to show prospective buyers around, and when you do receive an offer, handle any negotiations yourself. However, the whole process should save you money, although potential buyers will expect to be able to buy slightly cheaper as they realise that you won't have to pay commission to an agent.

If your house won't sell

In the property world, price is everything. And the main reason why a house proves difficult to sell is if you insist on putting it on the market at too high a price. Even a run-down property in a less-than-desirable part of town will often sell quickly if it is priced correctly. So work hard to get the price right, which will improve your chance of selling quickly:

- Do not get too emotional – remember that your home is worth what someone will pay for it, not what you think it ought to be worth or what it was worth when house prices were higher
- Look in local estate agents' windows to get some idea of the price that homes are selling for in your immediate neighbourhood
- Remember that these prices are not really selling prices – they are asking prices. In the real world, homes will probably sell for less than this
- If you still haven't found a buyer, you will have to accept that selling your home yourself doesn't always work. So give yourself a set time to find a buyer yourself – say a month or six weeks

USING AN ESTATE AGENT

Estate agents take the work and worry away from you and have better ways of publicising the property, as well as having lists of potential buyers in your area. All these factors give them a good chance of selling your home for you.

However, choosing an estate agent is an art in itself. There are good, bad and indifferent ones, as in any field, and it is not always easy to tell which is which, especially if this is the first time you are selling your home. Ask perhaps three different agents to visit your property and advise you what price they think it should be marketed at. Don't be led into telling them what you are looking for – you want their expertise. Talking to estate agents will also be good practice for dealing with potential buyers in the future.

Make a Wise Move
- Let Us Help
Whether Buying or Selling, our aim is quite simple - to provide you with the best estate agency service.
ALLEN & HARRIS
MANNERS & HARRISON
McQUITTY/ROSS
WILLIAM BROWN
JONES & CHAPMAN
Swetenhams
Bagshaws
WILLIAM BROWN
WILLIAM BROWN
Shipways
BROWN & MERRY
CROWN & CO
ALLEN & HARRIS
Roger Platt
barnard marcus
FOX & SONS
FOX & SONS
GRIBBLE BOOTH & TAYLOR
These well-known, local names make up Royal SunAlliance's national estate agency network. Over 420 offices throughout the UK with professional, experienced staff offer you local knowledge with national backing ...
... whether you're moving five minutes or 500 miles away.
To find out how we can help you, ring for details of your nearest office:
0990 841236

Don't necessarily choose the agent who proposes the highest price. You could end up facing suggestions that you cut the price after it has been on the market fruitlessly for several months. It is much better to get a realistic price first time. Remember that buyers use their common sense too when they are house-hunting. If a house features a 'For Sale' board which has been there so long that it is taking root, they will nod knowingly to themselves and decide that there is something wrong with the house. The longer a house is on the market, the harder it becomes to sell. Also, don't insist that an estate agent puts it on the market at an unrealistic price – one, for example, based on what you paid back in 1990. Prices have fallen dramatically since then in many areas. If you do insist on an unrealistic price, the estate agent will take the job, but, reasonably enough, may not put much effort into marketing the property as he knows it is overpriced and therefore won't sell.

So ask the estate agent how he justifies the price. Has he sold many properties in that area recently? Talk to him, does he sound like he really knows the area? Try to find out who will be handling the sale if you give the firm the business – it is frustrating to deal with different people each time you phone, none of whom are really on top of the situation. You should be prepared to reduce your asking price as potential buyers expect you to come down slightly – but if you price it accurately in the first place, you should be able to get away with a small reduction and a quick sale. The estate agent will invariably suggest that you have a 'For Sale' board outside, although you're not obliged to. What estate agents charge you depends partly on where you are – they charge more in London than in the provinces, for example and it also depends on what the deal is. By law, estate agents have to tell you their charges when you sign up. There are two main types of selling agreement:

- Sole agency – which means you put it in one agent's hands. This is not the same as giving him 'sole selling rights' (see below)
- Multiple agency, where a group of agents compete to find you a buyer

You will have to sign a legal agreement, but make sure that you do not concede 'sole selling rights' – this means you have to pay commission even if you find a buyer yourself.

Sole agency costs less. A survey from the Woolwich Building Society found that average sole agency bills were 2 per cent of the price, compared with 2.8 per cent for multiple agency. Like all averages they conceal variations – selling is usually more expensive in London than in the provinces, for example. You can always negotiate on these fees, but remember that you get what you pay for – an estate agent who is a skilled and experienced negotiator will more than compensate for an extra half a per cent on his fee.

Many sellers still choose multiple agency, on the basis that with several agents on the job, they will find a buyer more quickly. You have to bear in mind that agents are only human and they may put less effort into pushing your property if they risk losing the commission to a rival firm. If you are determined to go down this route, resist the temptation to choose two or three agents from the same area. Buyers visit them all collecting particulars and are likely to see your home several times. This will make them wonder what's wrong with it and will lead to low offers you'll find hard to improve upon. Instead, it makes sense to choose one agent in the area where you live, and two in neighbouring areas; one more up-market, and one down-market. That way you will also get potential buyers trading up or down. Even if you go for multiple agency, you will not be able to put up a 'For Sale' board from each agent, as it is now illegal to have more than one big or two small boards outside your house. In practice, it is not a good idea to have more than one board up. It cheapens your home, and makes potential buyers think there is something wrong with it.

Some buyers consider that you might find that you get better service from a well-established independent firm, where the partners are intimately involved with the neighbourhood, than from one of the big chains, even though the big chains can exchange information between different branches.

When you find a buyer, a good estate agent should handle much of the negotiating for you. He is – or should be – an experienced professional skilled in the arts of bluff and counter-bluff. This means, among other things, that he is less likely to let nerves get the better of him as an inexperienced seller can easily do.

The agent is obliged to put all offers to you and will add his opinion of them. Don't necessarily be panicked into accepting the first offer that comes along – your estate agents will probably advise against this as well. A potential buyer is expected to pitch his first offer low in the expectation that he will have to increase it later.

A good agent will probably be able to show potential buyers round during the day or at weekends. This is a major plus for the busy seller as you don't have to tie up your weekends or take time off work. To help this process, leave the keys with him, so he can take people to visit when you're away. This also means you won't have to take time off work when a buyer's surveyor wants to inspect.

Give an estate agent a fixed time to prove himself. If no viewers appear, ask why – perhaps he isn't pushing the property hard enough, or perhaps it's overpriced. If viewers still don't appear, don't hesitate to switch agents. If your home does not attract offers in the first month or so, consider lowering the price if you are keen to sell. It can be worth putting your home on the market at an optimistic price initially in the hope you will find a buyer willing to pay the price. But if this does not work, consider reducing the asking price. This can give agents a persuasive line to use on potential buyers, as they can say 'this house has just been reduced in price for a quick sale'.

GETTING YOUR HOUSE READY TO SELL

However good your agent, it is up to you to make the property as saleable as possible. It won't just make it easier to find a buyer in the first place, it will help you to get a better price. But don't do a comprehensive redecoration – in the first place, it might make a potential buyer suspicious and, in any case, your taste may not be the same as theirs. But do get rid of the niggling little features which cumulatively, can put off buyers.

Here is a checklist of the things to do before you start the selling process:

- Tidy up the garden, and get rid of any weeds. Repaint the front door if necessary, as well as the window frames at the front. Make sure the front gate hangs properly. First impressions count for a lot, and a run-down appearance can put off a buyer or make him want to cut your price down

- Sort out irritants inside – dripping taps, doors that stick, dead light bulbs and broken electrical fittings
- Give the house a thoroughly good clean; steam clean the carpets, for example, and wash down the paintwork
- Keep the place reasonably tidy – not obsessively so, but old coffee cups lying around give a terrible impression, as does a sofa covered with cat hairs
- Remember that an uncluttered house gives a wonderful impression of space, which is a great selling point. So pack junk away
- Don't cook smelly foods before people arrive – smells linger in people's minds. If you smoke, give the house a good airing before showing it
- Fresh flowers on the table help to give a good impression
- Keep dogs and cats under control, and don't let children make too much of a row either
- Have paperwork ready so you can tell a buyer what the council tax bill is, how much it costs to heat, and whether any work you have had done is still under guarantee

When showing someone over your home give them a brief tour, pointing out any special features, especially ones which will remain, but don't talk non-stop at them: a good house sells itself. Afterwards, ask them if they have any questions – and be ready with answers to potentially tricky ones such as 'why are you moving' and 'what are the neighbours like?' Ask them if they would like to wander around on their own and before they go, invite them to visit again if they want. Remember to give them both your home and work phone numbers.

Sadly, not everyone is totally trustworthy – so remove any small but valuable objects that could easily be pocketed! And on the same theme, don't go on about the strength and quality of the security features in the home – it makes potential buyers think they might be moving to a crime-ridden ghetto.

Incidentally, if you're nervous about showing strangers round your home alone, get a neighbour or friend to sit in or, better still, tell the estate agent to accompany all viewers.

Don't push a potential buyer; if they're interested, they'll come back to you. Oddly enough, the enthusiastic couple who seemed very interested may vanish from your life while the silent ones who looked around in a perfunctory way might just come up with an offer!

All buyers are not equal, and a good estate agent will have a shrewd idea of whether a potential offer is likely to lead to a sale. First-time and cash buyers are worth their weight in gold because they do not have to sell a home first before they can complete. The same applies to someone who has already sold, and has decided to rent for a few months. A good agent will also be able to point the inexperienced buyer in the direction of legal and financial help which will speed up the entire business.

Your buyer will naturally want you to take the house off the market while the legal work chunters along. He will regard this as a sign of good faith, and you should agree to this unless you doubt that they are willing and able to buy. In a smooth running sale, you will get to know your buyer quite well, as they will need to make repeated visits to consider decoration and to make accurate measurements for furniture. They may also want craftsmen or builders to visit too, if they are planning major alterations. You should try to give them fair access. If you have any problems you will need to raise them with the buyer – as a matter of etiquette your seller's solicitor cannot discuss the matter with you. You will also need to to synchronise dates for exchanging contracts so that you sell the old home and buy the new on the same day: this will obviously depend on the people whose house you are buying.

THE SELLING PROCESS

The legal side of selling is much less complicated than it is for buying. This is because the buyer – or rather his solicitor – has to do most of the work. As soon as you have accepted an offer, you will need to exchange names and addresses of solicitors, and pass details of the sale to your solicitor. He or she will draw up a draft contract of sale, and it will be up to the buyer to do all the necessary searches and satisfy himself about your right to sell. However, you will need to have some paperwork handy for your lawyer – evidence of buildings insurance, and receipts for service charges if applicable, for example. You will have to answer the preliminary enquiries sent by the buyer's solicitor – and answer them honestly. Your solicitor will also arrange for the repayment of your existing mortgage – remember that you may have to pay redemption penalties, so factor these into your financial calculations.

REMEMBER ...

You will need to decide whether to find a buyer, then put in an offer, or vice versa?

- If you decide to sell the property yourself rather than through an estate agent, be realistic about pricing
- An estate agent should be a skilled negotiator, who will act on your behalf to secure the best price. He or she can also save you time and effort – showing people around during office hours or at the weekend, for example
- Don't necessarily go for the estate agent who offers the highest price – the property may take longer to sell, and potential buyers will be put off by a 'For Sale' sign which seems to have taken root!
- Don't be panicked into accepting the first offer made
- Attending to niggles like an untidy garden or a dripping tap will impress prospective purchasers, but don't redecorate the whole house – a bunch of fresh flowers could prove a worthwhile investment, though
- Be prepared for tricky questions – for example, the buyers may want to know about your neighbours
- Buyers will need reasonable access to your house during the lead up to the entry date

English
Scottish
System

13

BUYING IN SCOTLAND

BUYING property north of the border is radically different, due to the fact that Scotland has its own legal system with different historical roots to that south of the border. For one thing, the much criticised leasehold system does not exist and in a block of flats, all owners have a defined legal responsibility which is set out in the title deeds. For another, most homes are sold through High Street property centres run by groups of solicitors rather than through estate agents, although they do, of course, exist. Solicitors have an effective monopoly of the property business in eastern Scotland, though not in the west of the country.

English solicitors are not allowed to practice north of the border, just as Scottish solicitors cannot practice in England. This is a sensible rule as the two systems of law differ. But an Englishman moving there should ask his solicitor for a recommendation. Otherwise, ask your mortgage lender for a recommendation.

It is when you come to the actual buying process that you will really notice the difference between the two systems. In the window of any solicitors' property centre you will see that properties are generally offered on the basis of 'offers over' a stated figure, usually called the upset price. However, it doesn't necessarily mean that a bargain is in store; this price is likely to be a minimum set to encourage competitive bidding. However, fixed price offers are not unknown, especially for new homes where it is fixed by the builder.

There is another huge difference when you buy in Scotland; under Scottish law, a written offer, once accepted, and concluded, is binding on both parties. So there is no gazumping and no gazundering either. This is obviously a good thing – the fear of gazumping is a key factor in the stress that house-buying causes in England and Wales. But the down side is that you have to have everything arranged before you make your offer. This includes a firm mortgage offer, and the survey which your mortgage lender will demand as a condition of the loan.

As a result of all this, the stages in buying in Scotland are radically different to those in England, and events generally move much faster. These are the ten steps toward owning your dream house north of the border:

- Arrange your mortgage finance – many of the big name building societies have branches in Scotland, while the Dunfermline is the biggest Scottish society. Get provisional approval for the amount of money that you would like to borrow
- Warn your solicitors that you will soon be buying somewhere
- Start the house-hunting process. Find somewhere that you would like to buy, have a good look round as you would in England, agree with the seller what things you want to remain, and when you would like to

move. Oral agreements are not binding, so you are not committed yet

- Tell your solicitors about the deal. They will contact the solicitor for the seller who will 'note' your interest
- Go back to the building society with full details, and arrange for a survey to be carried out
- If the survey is satisfactory, and if you are 100 per cent sure of your mortgage finance, you can finally instruct your solicitor to make a formal written offer for the property. Your lawyer should do this for you, as this offer is naturally couched in technical legal language and, once accepted, will form a binding contract. It will specify exactly what you want to remain behind and when you want to move in, known in Scotland as the 'entry date'. It will also detail some legal matters, such as making sure that there are no planning requirements or unduly onerous title conditions, such as an intrusive right of way. The offer letter will also ensure that maintenance of common parts is shared on a fair basis, and that the seller will produce good title to the property. The entry date is usually four to six weeks after the missives have been concluded. Naturally, if you are selling at the same time as buying, both entry dates must coincide unless you want to arrange expensive bridging finance
- If more than one buyer is interested in the property, the owner's solicitors will hold what amounts to an auction and will give your solicitor a closing date for final offers. You will have to bid blind as you will not be told details of rival bids. Neither are you allowed to

bid at '£500 more than the highest offer'. This bidding processs is naturally a stressful one, but you are not entirely on your own. The big role that Scottish solicitors play in the property market means that they are likely to have a good idea of what property will actually fetch and will be very helpful in this situation. Your survey will also have given you a valuation

- Hope for the best. The wait will not be long and you will normally learn within an hour or so of the closing date whether you were successful or not. If you don't get the property, you lose your survey fee, which is the downside of the Scottish rule that bans gazumping
- If you win, the seller's solicitor will prepare a formal legal document accepting your offer to buy. The seller will also produce a property enquiry certificate, detailing roads, planning and statutory repair notices which affect the property. The letters of offer and acceptance are known as missives and form a binding legal contract, together with any adjustments clarifing offer and acceptance details
- 'Conclusion of missives' – this obliges you to buy and the seller to sell. This is why it is so important to be sure of your mortgage. Since you are still obliged to buy if the house burns down, it is your responsibility to insure the property. Your solicitor will then begin the conveyancing procedure which will transfer the legal title from the seller to you. This document is called the disposition

REMEMBER ...

- Properties are usually bought and sold through groups of solicitors, rather than estate agents
- Competitive bidding is encouraged by offering the property on the basis of 'offers over' a stated figure
- An accepted written offer is legally binding, so there is no gazumping or gazundering – this means you must already have your mortgage and survey arranged, and that the offer must be prepared by a lawyer
- If more then one buyer is interested, an auction may be held, with closed bids. Your solicitor could be very helpful here in coming up with a realistic figure
- Insure the house as soon as your offer is accepted – once you have reached this point, you will still have to buy it even if it burns down!

14

BUILDING YOUR OWN HOME

Finding that dream home can be a problem: in one house the ceilings are too low; in another there is no cellar; in yet another there are too few rooms. If you cannot find a home you are happy with, you can build your home to suit your exact needs. Each year some 20,000 people reject the look-alike new homes put up by builders in favour of their own tailor-made dwelling. Every year a growing army of self-builders either build their own homes from scratch, renovate a derelict property or convert a building, most often a barn, into a home.

The rewards of self-building are financial as well as emotional. Not only do you become the envy of the neighbourhood, but completed properties are usually worth 30 per cent more than the cost of building, renovating or converting them. However, it is not a simple process. The home must be designed, planning permission approved – a notoriously difficult process – and a mortgage found. All this takes time and effort and not a little patience. A common reaction from intrepid self-builders is that they wondered why they were doing it while the process dragged on, but were extremely pleased that they had once it was all finally over.

HOW TO BUILD YOUR OWN HOME

There are a number of steps that have to be gone through when you self-build. These can be time-consuming and frustrating, but need to be carried through.

- Affordability – work out how much you can afford and put it to one side. Be realistic about this: running out of money with a half-built house on your hands is no joke
- Buy some land – find a plot of land to build, renovate or convert your property on. Do not be tempted to buy a piece of land until you have checked out whether it already has, or will be able to get, planning permission

granted on it. Local authority planning departments will not shrink from demolishing a building put up in the wrong place or without their say-so

- Design your home – what you can do will depend first on whether there are any special covenants on the land that prevent it being used in certain ways. Land bought in conservation areas is particularly prone to such problems. Most people design their homes with the help of an architect, who should be able to guide you through this minefield. While this can save on the eventual cost of putting up your home, there will also be architect's fees to pay
- Planning permission – you must have planning permission before you start building. This has to be obtained from your local authority's planning department. According to many self-builders and architects this can be a lengthy and nightmarish procedure. Planning departments can often seem like a rule unto themselves. Try to find out early on what they are likely to object to on a particular plot of land or building and see if you can work your way around those problems. The alternative is to go back to the drawing board – and that takes time and money
- Builder – find a decent builder to do the work for you. Very few people have the time or the skill to lay their own bricks and mortar, or carry out conversion work. The rule is: shop around to see what can be provided at what cost, and check the timescale. Do not let your builder start work on the basis of a vague estimate of the cost. Tie your builder down to a firm cost and get a

written quotation. This means you will not get the nasty shock of an extra bill later on. If any extra work is necessary, make sure you get a written quotation for that too

The Associated Self-Build Architects recommends that you set aside an extra 5 per cent of the building costs to cover any unexpected eventualities if you are building a property from scratch. The element of the unexpected increases those costs for conversions and renovations and it suggests putting aside an extra 10 to 20 per cent for them.

HOW MUCH WILL IT COST?

Apart from the cost of buying your plot of land and paying for the property to be built or renovated, there is a host of other costs that need to be taken into consideration:

- Land – your plot will cost on average between one-third and a half of your total budget
- Building – the average cost is £40 to £45 per square foot. To get the total cost of building your home, multiply this by the size of the building
- Site survey – this will usually cost about £350
- Structural engineer's partial service – you need this to get building regulations approved. It costs between £400 and £500
- Planning and building regulations – a detailed planning application costs £160, and the two-stage building regulations cost £90 to £100 for the plan fee and then £210 to £220 for a further inspection fee
- Connection charges – connecting up to water, gas,

electricity and drainage will set you back about £2,000. Building guarantee insurance is a good idea, as it will pay out in the event of any disasters. This costs £500 to £1,000

- Professional fees – architect's fees on their own can amount to 8 to 10 per cent of the total cost. Solicitors' and surveyors' fees will depend on how much work they do and how complicated it is

RAISING THE CASH

Lenders are a little more wary of self-build projects than they are of ordinary homes. Very often the money is released in stages as the building work progresses. There is also a higher than average deposit required – usually 20 per cent of the cost of the whole project.

The mortgage will usually float on the lender's standard variable mortgage rate. However some lenders, such as the Ecology Building Society, offer a discount on that rate after a number of years.

The Department of the Environment publishes a guide to self-building called Planning – A Guide for Householders, available from the DoE, Publications Dispatch Centre, Blackhorse Road, London SE99 6TT.

REMEMBER ...

- Make sure you won't run out of money and be stuck with a half-built house – see our checklist of major costs, above
- Set aside a percentage of the building costs for unforeseen eventualities
- Check planning permission and restrictive covenants
- It is more vital than ever to find a good architect and a reliable builder
- Getting a mortgage could be tricky – often, lenders will release money for self-build projects in stages
- You will probably doubt your sanity during the process, but most self-builders are glad they did it – once it's all over
- Self-build can be financially as well as emotionally rewarding

USEFUL ADDRESSES

The Association of British Insurers (ABI)
51 Gresham Street
London EC2V 7HQ
Tel: 0171 600 3333

The Association of Relocation Agents
Premier House
11 Marlborough Place
Brighton BN1 1VB
Tel: 01273 624455

Associated Self-Build Architects
Junction 41
Business Court
East Arsley
West Yorkshire WS3 2AB
Tel: 0800 387310

Banking Ombudsman
70 Gray's Inn Road
London WC1X 8NB
Tel: 0171 404 9944

The British Association of Removers (BAR)
3 Churchill Court
58 Station Road
North Harrow
Middlesex HA2 7SA
Tel: 0181 861 3331

The British Insurance and Investment Brokers Association (BIIBA)
BIIBA House
14 Bevis Marks
London EC3A 7NT
Tel: 0171 623 9043

Building Employers Confederation
82 New Cavendish Street
London W1M 8AD
Tel: 0171 580 5588

The Building Societies Association/Council of Mortgage Lenders (BSA/CML)
3 Savile Row
London W1X 1AF
Tel: 0171 437 0655

Building Societies Ombudsman
Millbank Tower
Millbank
London SW1P 4XS
Tel: 0171 931 8485

Conservatory Council
Glass and Glazing Federation
44–48 Borough High Street
London SE1 1XB
Tel: 0171 403 7177

Council for Licensed Conveyancers (CLC)
16 Glebe Road
Chelmsford
Essex CM1 1QG
Tel: 01245 349599

Department of the Environment

1) Public Enquiry Point
Room P2/162
2 Marsham Street
London SWIP 3EB
Tel: 0171 276 0900

2) Publications Dispatch Centre
Blackhorse Road
London SE99 6TT

The Federation of Master Builders (FMB)
14 Great James Street
London WC1V 3DP
Tel: 0171 242 7583

The Housing Corporation
149 Tottenham Court Road
London W1P 0BN
Tel: 0171 393 2000

The Incorporated Society of Valuers and Auctioneers (ISVA)
3 Cadogan Gate
London SW1X 0AS
Tel: 0171 235 2282

Insurance Brokers
Registration Council
15 St Helens Place
London EC3A 6DS
Tel: 0171 588 4387

Insurance Ombudsman
Bureau
135 City Gate One
London SE1 9EA
Tel: 0171 928 4488

The Law Society
113 Chancery Lane
London WC2A 1PL
Tel: 0171 242 1222

The Law Society of Scotland
26 Drumsheugh Gardens
Edinburgh EH3 7YR
Tel: 0131 226 7411

The Leasehold Advisory
Service
8 Maddox Street
London W1R 9PN
Tel: 0171 493 3116

The National Association of
Estate Agents (NAEA)
Arbon House
21 Jury Street
Warwick CV34 4EH
Tel: 01926 496800

The National House
Building Council (NHBC)
Buildmark House
Chiltern Avenue
Amersham
Buckinghamshire HP6 5AP
Tel: 01494 434477

National Housing
Federation
175 Gray's Inn Road
London WC1X 8UP
Tel: 0171 278 6571

National Approval Council
for Security Systems
(NACoSS)
Queensgate House
14 Cookham Road
Maidenhead
Berkshire SL6 8AJ
Tel: 01628 37512

The New Homes Marketing
Board (NHMB)
82 New Cavendish Street
London W1M 8AD
Tel: 0171 580 5588

Office for the Supervision of
Solicitors (OSS)
Victoria Court
8 Dormer Place

Leamington Spa
Warwickshire CV32 5AE
Tel: 01926 820082

Office of Legal Services Ombudsman
22 Oxford Court
Oxford Street
Manchester M2 3WQ
Tel: 0161 236 9532

Registry of County Court Judgments
173–175 Cleveland Street
London W1P 5PE
Tel: 0171 380 0133

The Royal Institute of British Architects (RIBA)
Clients' Advisory Service
66 Portland Place
London W1N 4AD
Tel: 0171 580 5533

The Royal Institution of Chartered Surveyors (RICS)
12 Great George Street
London SW1P 3AD
Tel: 0171 222 7000

The Royal Institution of Chartered Surveyors in Scotland (RICS Scotland)
9 Manor Place
Edinburgh EH3 7DN
Tel: 0131 225 7078

For independent financial advisers, many of whom can give mortgage advice, contact:

IFA Promotion
17–19 Emery Road
Brislington
Bristol BS4 5PF
Tel: 0117 971 1177

INDEX

INDEX OF ADVERTISERS